GOD
SKY
MAZE 1
Andrew / Malka

PEARL SMITHERN

God Sky Maze 1
Copyright © 2023 by Pearl Smithern

Printed in the United States of America.

ISBN
979-8-88945-240-9 (Paperback)
979-8-88945-241-6 (eBook)

Brilliant Books Literary
137 Forest Park Lane Thomasville
North Carolina 27360 USA

I wish to thank FIRST (MY LORD), my beautiful children: Carol, Robert, Karen Cunningham and Sharon Caldwell.

Thanks to all my other friends that prayed and gave encouraging words. The home schoolers and students who said the book will be a plus in their teaching. Wayland Church in Ravenna, Ohio are waiting for it to be on sale.

Ruby Pautz, sister—for the hours of listening to me. Steve Stein, Ruby's son- on proofing poem.

Janice Wymer, sister—her reminders to check spelling.

Daniel Tkach-son in law—for the pictures and for his mother's handiwork. Mary Stanton—** Edit, proofing and research

PART I

1

*Maybe *Christmas Play Material**

The birth of Jesus as told in Luke 2:1-15. Once a long time ago when the shepherds were watching their flocks by night, there appeared a bright star and angels praising God and saying, "Glory to God in the highest, and on earth peace to men on whom his favor rests." The shepherds said one to another, "Let's go to Bethlehem and see this thing that has happened, which the Lord has told us about." They came with haste and found Mary and Joseph with the babe lying in a manger.

One shepherd boy, Simon, stayed behind. He wanted a closer look at the babe, and somehow, he was going to get another look.

The little room became quiet and still except for the noise of the animals settling down for the night. Mary lifted the little babe to her bosom and sang a lovely song as she cradled him back and forth in her arms: "The foxes have holes and the birds of the air have nests, but the little babe has nowhere to lay his head, nowhere to lay his head." Mary kissed him tenderly and tucked the cloth around his little feet so that they would stay warm through the night. Mary then blew out the candles and, lying down on the straw mat, soon was fast asleep.

Simon, hiding behind the stall, moved the cow's foot as it was getting closer to his. He couldn't afford noise now, *not now!* The time was right for moving toward the manger and getting another look. Oh, how his heart pounded within his breast. How the thoughts ran through his mind. Was his uncle looking for him? Were his sheep missing the sound of his voice? Would he receive another correction from the rod?

I can't dwell on this now, he thought. *I've got to move quietly and slowly toward the manger, got to keep pressing in.* Simon shuffled with his elbows and knees across the straw.

Wait…where was that small beam of light coming from? Simon looked through the darkness with all the strength his little eyes could muster. Was another candle left burning? Maybe Joseph was still awake.

Simon suddenly felt afraid and foolish. He thought, *If I get caught, what would I say—a big boy wanting to touch a little baby? Why, they would ask? I have other siblings at home and crying cousins here in Bethlehem. Then why?*

Simon felt gripped in his very being to come near the babe. The angels had sung, so he knew that the babe was special. He was to become a king and when he smiled at all of them earlier…*wow*. He noticed the light continued to shine softly on into the night and seemed to be coming from the manger itself.

Moving now among the sheep that crowded in his corner, making it harder for him to hide, he crawled on his stomach through the hay and found it was not at all pleasant. Soon Simon was just an arm's length away from the babe. He could hear a coo and then a laugh. He smiled to himself and wondered why this babe was still awake when all else were asleep.

Simon cautiously got up on his knees, peeking his face over the manger. The look of the babe gazing at him was worth all the fear of waiting and worth the whipping, if he got one, for not coming home.

Simon whispered sweet words to the babe and then noticed something hidden down in the straw. It was softly glowing. So the light was coming from the manger. He pulled the straw back and lifted up a small star beam.

"How did you get here?" Simon asked quietly.

It answered, "My name is Maybe, and I came in on the shepherd's staff when the angels were singing and the light was shooting beams down to announce the glorious event. I got carried away with the excitement and got too close to the earth, like a falling star. I caught hold of the staff of the tallest shepherd. When his staff was laid down, I fell into the manger right at the babe's feet."

Simon put the star beam into his pocket, promising the little babe he would take good care of it. He leaned farther into the manger and kissed the little babe on the forehead and then on the little hands that were reaching upward to him.

Were those stories true? Would those very same hands be scarred for him? For his people? Simon felt a teardrop enter his eyes. How could he be filled with joy and sorrow all at the same time? Simon whispered, "No, I won't cry."

He knew about being lonely and afraid. Some nights on the hills of Judea, he would weep because of the loss of his mother. He could still hear her singing and smell the aroma of the warm bread filling the house. Things just were not the same now. He had to drop out of school to help his uncle with the sheep earning some wages while Andrew is helping father with the fishing business. His older sister was engaged to be married. She was wonderful, but she wasn't mother.

Simon lowered himself down again onto his stomach and shuffled toward the doorway. The star beam lit the way for his feet as he headed toward the hills and to his lonely life. With sad countenance, Simon sighed, "I'd rather be back in Capernaum, fishing."

As he reached the camp, he tucked Maybe down into his tattered cloth sandal so that the light would not give them away. He saw that his uncle was asleep. Little did Simon know that his uncle knew all along that he had stayed behind. Simon's head was filled with many thoughts as he drifted off to sleep. One thought was about Maybe, and another was that the light shouldn't be kept hidden. Simon didn't know that an angel was lifting Maybe out of his sandal and into the angel's hand, all the while filling Simon's head with a promise dream: "I lift up my eyes to the hills—where does my help come from?" (Ps. 121:1).

"And you little Maybe," said the angel, "know your Father sees even when a sparrow falls. What? You want to be the North Star. You like helping a traveler home. Well—maybe?"

Smiling toward the earth, the angel said, "Sweet dreams to all and to all look up, look north."

2

Shepherd's Chill

A chill was all around us like a blanket tight.
Our breath vapors caught by the flickering firelight.
Strong sounds of night penetrated the surrounding air,
Heard even by those lying in pairs.
Mother ewes snuggled their babies few,
Keeping them from the creeping dew.
Even the rams noticed the chill
And laid closer into the hill.
Restlessness and the sound of their bleating
Made us adjust our camp seating.
We placed cold hands into our pockets.
Our toes in our robes wrapped up like lockets.
Then the sky came open with angelic delight,
Singing angels telling why with heavenly might.
Like rain drops each note fell,
Into this musical saga without a yell.
"Peace on earth, goodwill to men,"
However, there was no room to put Him in.
In a stable, wrapped with swaddling cloth,
As told in the Christmas story, we're all taught.
Science has said that outer space is cold,
Maybe explaining when the sky opened a hole
For angelic heralding of Immanuel's birth,
A Shepherd's chill was felt all over the earth.[*]

* Good homework fun for around the season time.

3

Quiz-Smarts

Have Fun
Use Poem Shepherds Chill

Questions:	Answers:
1. What made vapors?	2
2. How did the notes fall for musical saga	3
3. What are we taught?	4
4. What two words can be changed by the first letter and be the same?	1
5. What came out of the open sky?	6
6. What did the mother ewes keep from the babies?	5

1. Locket and pocket
2. Breath
3. Like rain drops each note
4. Christmas story *Wrapped
5. Creeping dew
6. Singing angel-angelic heralding

*Also If you said chill came out of the sky, give yourself a high-five

SPECIAL QUESTION FOR EVERYONE
- WHO WAS BORN ON CHRISTMAS DAY?
- IF YOU WERE "HAPPY BIRTHDAY"

4

Barabbas *Easter Play Material*

What would a man like this think? When on the Feast of Passover with thousands of pilgrims coming to Jerusalem, the Roman authorities released him, a man who belongs to the group of feared zealots, thought Pilate.

Pilate heard the crowd shouting, "Release to us Barabbas. Release to us Barabbas." Barabbas knew what he was. He knew his crimes: a robber, a murderer, insurrectionist, and a notorious prisoner. But now he was riding for his life to leave Jerusalem, for no one knew what that crazy crowd would do next.

Inside Barabbas' head, his thoughts wondered about this man called Jesus, a man who would let Himself be beaten and bruised and yet not speak a word—like a weak one. He remembered how a few of the guards ended up with broken arms and one with a broken jaw the day of his capture. They knew what he was like and remembered it for days. What he saw in Jesus made him shake his head.

He kept up a good pace with the camel and wondered if his men were still holed up at their favorite hideout, the inn. His heart had really turned to stone, and he could have cared less as he struck his camel into a faster trot and let out a loud laugh. *Oh, those chief priests and elders. You are one for the books, choosing me over a good man,* he thought. *A few days in Egypt would be the best plan for a while. Then my good Romans, I shall return.* His laughter echoed against the change coming on the edge of the day.

He shuddered as the sky grew dark, and the earthquake startled the camel into a run. Barabbas jerked it to a halt so hard the camel buckled to its knees, and they both rolled onto the ground with a cursing oath coming forth from Barabbas. "I would kill you right now you ugly beast, except the thought of crossing the desert on foot is not appealing even for this mighty zealot."

Little did he know that the terror of the sky and the earthquake was being felt in Jerusalem, as well, the third hour of the day when a seemingly weak Man was giving up His Spirit for the sins of the world.

PART II

1

Simon

Bethsaida (meaning house of fish), my native town, is located on the western coast of the Sea of Galilee. That's where my youth was spent since coming back from attending sheep for my uncle in Bethlehem.

My father was Jacob Barjona and my mother was Joanna, and I am Simon Barjona. It is just a common Jewish name meaning "hearing." But I didn't hear the illness in my mother's voice the last time we talked nor realized what dangers awaited on that beautiful sea.

Soon my uncle took me home to help in the family since mother wanted it that way, great working at fishing is not work for me after sheep, love you mom. Andrew and I knew Salome and her husband Zebedee along with their two sons James and John. Those two boys had to settle everything, well almost everything, by arm wrestling, and, you guessed it, when they messed with me I usually won.

I was growing strong in body and height, which pretty much made me the leader when it came to what we were going to do, unless I really made them angry. Then I could hear the thunder; in fact, Andrew and I started calling them Boanerges, which means Sons of Thunder.

Zebedee was a man of position in Capernaum, for he had two boats and "hired servants" of his own. He helped me to get my own boat, and this increased our livelihood. I thought, *Great, now I can get married, and we can have our own home in Capernaum.*

Right away, Salome started giving me and Andrew religious training in accordance with the Torah and with the great prophecies. But I was a Galilean, and we had a marked character of our own. We had the reputation for being independent and energetic, which often ran out into turbulence. We were sometimes blunt, impetuous, headstrong, and simple. Yes, I was a genuine Galilean. We even spoke a peculiar dialect. The guttural sounds and pronunciations were harsh in Judea. We couldn't hide where we had grown up.

Growing up in Bethsaida meant living near the shores of the Sea of Galilee. The Sea of Galilee is oval shaped and abounds in fish, so fishing is the prominent occupation. Many other fishing villages dot the Galilean shore, including Tiberias and Capernaum.

This sea has been in my blood from the time my father taught me to skip a rock across the waves; however, fishing a sea of twelve and a half miles long and four to seven and a half miles broad can be and is exhausting, especially the days I would catch nothing.

I remember the first time I saw Anna. She was down by the fishing boat one warm and sunny day. I didn't even know who she was or where she lived. She was so beautiful and small compared to my huge stature, but she could throw the pebbles and rocks across the waves like a guiding rope, skipping and skipping. Then when her arm came back, the pebbles would sink beneath the waves. I might add that she was almost as good as I.

When she saw me, she left just as fast as she could. I guess she was letting me know she didn't like me. Courting is like fishing—sometimes a good one gets away. I remember her remarks about my language being coarse as she turned to leave, more running than walking. I thought, *Someone should tame that one. I talk like the sailor I am, a big, Galilean fisherman. Dear lady, I assure you…I'm not changing.*

My father was in love with the sea first. It was he that gave me the first fishing line and hook. He showed me how to bait and clean and make my nets taut and to keep them clean. He talked about how the sea could change and how the storms could appear out of nowhere. *Ahhh, where have the years gone?*

Andrew lanky and manly is now staying with us since we lost our father. He had not even considered getting married. He was always sneaking away and going out to the desert to listen to preaching from a man who dressed like a wild man and ate locust and wild honey. It was upsetting to me, especially when I needed him to help me on fishing nights. Didn't he realize that fishing was our livelihood? In addition, Anna wasn't feeling well. I hoped the God of Abraham could see my future.

Mending, washing, drying, and then folding the nets were part of the never-ending jobs involved with fishing, and the better fisherman was known by his care of the boats and equipment. John was great at mending nets. I think he could tie knots with his eyes closed. There is danger involved; however, so we sometimes swim naked to avoid getting tangled up in the nets and drowning.

We used the oldest type of nets on our boats called dragnets. This net is up to three hundred feet long, sometimes requiring up to sixteen men to handle the load. The fish then had to be sorted. This process was repeated up to eight times a day, making a long, exhausting but pleasurable day. Another type of net, the cast net, was great, too. It was a circular net thrown by one man, which took great skill. Andrew was very good at this type of fishing, but I might add, I am better.

Andrew was caring less and less about fishing now because his interest was growing in the one called John the Baptist, who had begun preaching in the countryside of the Jordan River and in the desert area. Andrew had become a follower. A woman to attract his mind I could have understood, but a wild locust-eating screaming man?

Andrew in Greek means manly and brave; I could have changed that to idler and dreamer of dreams. Running with Philip and his Greek friends was not helping the situation. However, he did live up to his name when he helped my Anna during the very hard labor and consoled her mother when the child was born too early. Where was I on that frightful day? Oh, yes, in the middle of the sea. Andrew comforted me with words. Yes, you guessed it, from that John the Baptist. He told me that there was coming a kingdom where we all would be together. Cry—no, not the big fisherman. I was sure that more children would be born later.

Times were changing. The news among us was about the Roman rulers such as Herod Antipas, Tiberius, and Caligula, all lovers of luxury, all going into Tiberias for the baths and elaborate spa treatments. Meanwhile, taxes were being increased on the fishing leases and products; in addition, tolls had been increased on cartage and shipping. The people murmured among themselves behind closed doors. I shared a few points myself. Down several roads, outlaws could be seen hanging on crosses. Everyone thought that peace would come to us if only the Romans could be ousted out of Israel.

Following John the Baptist was becoming harder to do as he had offended Herod because of Herod's marriage, so John had been arrested. I cautioned Andrew, but he kept on going to the meetings and staying the night. And then—the news. John (clothed in camel's hair, a leather belt around his waist, and eating locust and wild honey), we heard, had been beheaded. Andrew stayed closer to home after that and was very quiet. I felt he was trying to put the pieces together. He came to faith through John and believed that a new kingdom was coming—a kingdom that would be peaceful and loving with people being good to one another.

I remember Andrew telling me about one incident when John the Baptist talked to the Pharisees and Sadducees and called them a brood of vipers. He kept talking about the one who was coming after him, who was mightier than him, whose sandals he was not worthy to carry. He preached that this one would baptize with the Holy Spirit and fire. The religious leaders thought he was demon possessed.

Andrew was there the day that Jesus, came down to the Jordan to be baptized. Andrew said immediately when He came up from the water, the heavens were opened, and God descended like a dove and alighted upon Him. Then Jesus quickly left and went into the wilderness.

Now, we thought, where was all this going? Little did we know that this Jesus was coming from Nazareth to the regions of Zebulun and Naphtali. We didn't know that this Jesus would be walking by the Sea of Galilee and would soon change both of our lives.

Jesus, when He saw us, said, "Come, follow me, and I will make you fishers of men" (Matt. 4:19). We immediately left our nets and followed Him. Going on from there, He saw James and John, the sons of Zebedee, mending their nets. He called them, and they left the boat and their father, and we all followed Him. Jesus said He had heard about John being put into prison. He said that now He would begin preaching, "Repent, for the Kingdom of Heaven is near" (Matt. 3:2).

"What! I'm a follower?" I remember thinking.

Jesus began preaching at the synagogues, healing all kinds of sicknesses and all kinds of diseases among the people. Then His fame grew from Jerusalem and beyond the Jordan. Andrew became a believer of Jesus back when he recognized Jesus as the Messiah, but we did not fully follow the Lord until after John's imprisonment and death. Andrew talked about the miracle of feeding the five thousand. He was there to bring the lad with the loaves to Jesus. He talked about some of Philip's Greek friends. He had been the one to take them to Jesus.

Andrew had a loving, kind, caring nature about him, and now I'm sorry for the tongue-lashings I gave him about having his head always in the clouds dreaming. He loved the Lord and was very brave, and he was a believer. He knew before I did that Jesus was the Messiah. I should have recognized Him. I should have remembered that night long ago on the Judean hills when I attended my uncle's sheep. Andrew kept telling me, "Simon, I have found the Messiah." I could not yet fully comprehend this mentally and was, I guess, totally lost for understanding.

The next day Jesus found Philip and Nathanael. On the third day, we went to a wedding in Cana of Galilee. I guess that was the day I somewhat began to believe in Him. Water, into wine! Unbelievable!

Jesus came and stayed many times at my home in Capernaum. In fact, my home became known as the fisherman's house. One time I had spent all night fishing on that cantankerous sea and came up unsuccessfully when Jesus suddenly appeared and entered into my boat. He bade me to launch forth and to let down the nets. I said, "Master, we've worked hard all night and haven't caught anything. But because you say so, I will let down the nets" (Luke 5:5). The nets were so full they began breaking, and I had to signal to my partners in the other boats to come and help me. Both the boats began to sink. I fell down at Jesus's knees saying, "Go away from me, Lord; I am a sinful man!" (Luke 5:8). Jesus said that from now on I would be catching men.

When we brought the boats to land, I forsook the fishing trade and told my family that from now on I would be following Jesus, having been called into the stormy seas of humanity, catching men for the Lord. Little did I know I was being called into the leading events of our Lord's life. The most difficult time came when He was teaching at the synagogue in Capernaum and spoke the hard saying that made many disciples leave and go back to walk with Him no more. Then Jesus said to us (the twelve), "You do not want to leave too, do you?" (John 6:67). I answered Him, "Lord, to whom shall we go? You have the words of eternal life. We believe and know that you are the Holy One of God" (John 6:68-69). When He began teaching us about the things He must suffer, I took Him aside and began to rebuke Him, but after He turned and looked at His disciples, He rebuked me, saying, "Get behind me, Satan! You are a stumbling block to me; you do not have in mind the things of God, but the things of men"

(Matt. 16:23). I knew I had yet to learn many things; yes, this was every bit as hard as rowing a boat in a terrible storm. His stern words to me cut right into my very being. Did He notice my anger; did He notice as my hand ran over my sword? I hoped not.

Because of the rigid rules I had to follow as a fisherman, life had taught me not to quit. If in transporting our catch, the fish dried out, we would have suffered loss, so we had to continually keep water on them until we reached our destination. We traveled to places such as Tiberias, Capernaum, or other cities where the fish would be taken by mules to a seaport city so the catch could be loaded onto ships and taken to Rome. Our fish was also popular in Damascus and in Jerusalem among the priestly crowd. Since John knew the high priest Caiaphas, we supplied fish for his family.

Sometimes we took our fish to Magdala to be dried and cured. In Aramaic Magdala means "Tower of Fish," but in the Greek it means "dried fish." While there, on occasion we would explore this famous city on the western coast of the Sea of Galilee. Then we began to hear rumors of a certain woman called Mary Magdalene, who was demon possessed. We certainly didn't want to cross her path, so we curtailed our explorations.

I didn't know that learning to fish for men would take up to three years or more; however, I knew that I wasn't a quitter. I wondered if Jesus would see this in me. I wanted him to. One thing was for sure, Jesus had to know that I had some good qualities that I learned while fishing for fish. Fishing caused me to be strong and hard-working, patient, and sociable. I wish I had been more fortunate when it came to my schooling.

Fish, a staple food, was depended upon for my living. Now I had exchanged fishing for the Word of the Master and for His kingdom. The kingdom ministry became my new life.

2

Ministry with Messiah

Home visits were few and far between as I started to go with Jesus wherever His Father (God) directed Him. Jesus had begun to tell us about the Father, and everything He did was the direct cause of obeying His Father.

My mother-in-law, after Jesus healed her, was better than ever (Matt. 8:14-15). She wanted to travel to Gadara to see about Anna, but I told her that she must not travel now under any terms, especially going it all alone at her age and with the upheaval. Who was to know what would happen. I knew that made her heart heavy.

My lovely, strong, and independent wife, however, could handle anything that was happening in her life. For example, when I told Jesus that I would leave all to follow Him, Anna and I both knew that following the Master was of primary importance. She knew that lonely times would surely come but was prepared to sacrifice.

Jesus comforted us by saying, "I tell you the truth...no one who has left home or brothers or sisters or mother or father or children or fields for me and the gospel will fail to receive a hundred times as much in this present age (homes, brothers, sisters, mothers, children and fields—and with them, persecutions) and in the age to come, eternal life (Mark 10:29-30). Persecutions—that was the part I had begun to understand all too well. I remember Anna's demanding voice directed right at me when I left my dirty fishing gear and tangled nets along with my sandals at the door. Thank goodness for a good mother- in-law that helped the tall, proud fisherman.

Multitudes now had begun to run on foot from all cities to hear and see Jesus.

He began teaching many things. The crowds moved Him with compassion for them because they were like sheep not having a shepherd.

For instance, one day He fed over five thousand people with a few loaves and fishes.

What a miracle! (Matt. 14:13-21).

How well I remember this. Right after He sent the multitudes away, we got into our boat to go to the other side (Matt. 14:22-27). We were out in our boat without Him and right in the middle of the sea when the winds became contrary and began tossing the boat around. He came to us walking on the sea. We cried out, "It's a ghost!" (Matt. 14:26).

But I, the big fisherman—right—spoke to Jesus and said, "Lord, if it's you...tell me to come to you on the water" (Matt. 14:28).

So He said, "Come" (Matt. 14:29). I came down out of the boat and started walking toward Him; then a wave hit my hip, and the water splashed into my face for the wind was boisterous.

Afraid, yes, I became afraid and started sinking. Did I cry out? Yes, I cried out, "Lord, save me!" (Matt. 14:30).

Immediately, Jesus stretched out His hand to me and caught me, then said, "You of little faith... why did you doubt me?" (Matt. 14:31). "Take courage! It is I. Don't be afraid" (Mark 6:50). We were greatly amazed beyond measure, for who is this that even the wind and waves obey? Yes, where was my faith? I decided to show Jesus I could be a good disciple.

Just touching the hem of His garment was healing many (Luke 8:45). Sometimes it was all we could do to keep Jesus from being mobbed by reaching hands and pressing bodies.

In Caesarea, Philippi, I was told by Jesus I had a revelation from His Father on who men said He was. I boldly answered, "You are the Christ, the Son of the Living God" (Matt. 16:16). Then He mentioned about building His church on The Rock (Christ), giving the keys of the kingdom to the church. He commanded us to tell no one.

When we had come to Capernaum, those who received the temple tax came to me and said, "Doesn't your teacher pay the temple tax?" (Matt. 17:24). Jesus then asked me what I thought. Was He a Son or a stranger? I told Him that we take our taxes to strangers. Then He taught me not to offend authority and said, "Go down to the sea and throw in a line. Open the mouth of the first fish you catch, and you will find a large silver coin. Take it and pay the tax for both of us" (Matt. 17:27).

Did I remember how to bait and cast. Come on musht—bite. It was spring and, of course, my human thought was the bigger the fish the bigger the coin. Knowing the habit of the musht, I understood that in the spring musht swallow coins and pebbles to make the baby fish uncomfortable so that they would swim on their own. Would not Jesus who created all things know this, too? Nevertheless, I got real pleasure out of casting again and catching that fish. It was in my blood.

The day we drew near Jerusalem and came to Bethphage on the Mount of Olives, Jesus said to John and Matthew, "Go to the village ahead of you, and at once you will find a donkey tied there, with her colt by her. Untie them and bring them to me. (Matt: 21:2-3) They brought the donkey Marni and the colt, Aliza, laid their clothes on them and set Jesus on Aliza. A great multitude spread their clothes on the road; others cut down branches from the trees and spread them on the road. The crowds that went ahead of Him and those that followed shouted, "Hosanna to the Son of David!" "Blessed is he who comes in the name of the Lord!" "Hosanna in the highest!" (Matt. 21:9). I yelled to the last inch of all my breath.

Jesus entered the temple area and drove out all who were buying and selling there. He overturned the tables of the moneychangers and the benches of those selling doves. He said to them, "It is written…'My house will be called a house of prayer,' but you are making it a 'den of robbers'" (Matt. 21:13). My heart was in my throat all the while He did this. We then left and went out of the city to Bethany. My sword was still in its sheath. Whew!

When Jesus was in the house of Simon the leper, a woman came to him having an alabaster flask of precious oil, and she poured it on His head and on His feet (Matt. 26:6- 13). Again, He mentioned that this was for His burial. But because Judas said, "What a waste of money," I talked to him about cooling his attitude and his indignant manner. My heart remembered Jesus talking about what was to come in the way of suffering and smelling that perfume and seeing those tears made me feel so useless. Not even the feel of my sword helped.

Judas—one of us—how could he? He was waiting for the opportunity to betray Jesus. Judas went to the chief priest and for thirty pieces of silver betrayed the Master (Matt. 26:15). Why didn't I see this…why didn't I stop the betrayal? As is later evident, the great, strong, and courageous fisherman was a coward.

The Passover came, and we celebrated in an upper room (Matt. 26:17-25). Judas left in a hurry like always. He was unhappy about something. Jesus, however, knew where Judas was going.

Jesus took the wine and the bread and began teaching us about a new covenant, causing my heart to keep failing within me. But I held back the tears. Cry? Not this big fisherman.

Then Jesus took off His outer clothing, and taking a towel, He wrapped it around His waist. Then He poured water into a bowl to wash our feet, drying them with the towel that was wrapped around Him. When Jesus came to me, I said, "No…you shall never wash my feet."

He answered me, looking directly into my eyes, "Unless I wash you… you have no part with me" (John 13:8).

"Then, Lord…not just my feet but my hands and my head as well!" (John 13:10).

Jesus replied, "A person who has had a bath needs only to wash his feet; his whole body is clean. And you are clean, though not every one of you" (John 13:10). Jesus knew who was going to betray Him and that was why He told us that not everyone was clean. He explained that no servant is greater than his master, nor is a messenger greater than the one who sent him, but now that we knew these things, we would be blessed if we did them. Little did I know that later in my life I would understand the complete meaning of being a good and faithful servant.

Jesus told us that He was going away. I asked, "Lord, where are you going?" (John 13:36). And Jesus replied, "Where I am going, you cannot follow now, but you will follow later" (John 13:36).

"Lord, why can't I follow you now? I will lay down my life for you," I asked (John 13:37).

Jesus answered, "Will you really lay down your life for me? I tell you the truth, before the rooster crows, you will disown me three times!" (John 13:38).

Three times! I thought, Never, *I'm the big fisherman.*

Jesus then turned His attention to Thomas. Thomas asked Him about how we could know the way. Jesus replied, "I am the way, the truth, and the life" (John 14:6).

Then Philip said to Him, "Lord, show us the Father, and that will be enough for us" (John 14:8). Jesus replied, "Don't you know me, Philip, even after I have been among you such a long time? Anyone who has seen me has seen the Father. How can you say, 'Show us the Father'?" (John 14:9). He explained that He and His Father are one.

Jesus promised us another helper.

If you love me, you will obey what I command. And I will ask the Father, and he will give you another Counselor to be with you forever—the Spirit of truth. The world cannot accept him, because it neither sees him nor knows him. But you know him, for he lives with you and will be in you. I will not leave you as orphans; I will come to you. Before long, the world will not see me anymore, but you will see me. Because I live, you also will live. On that day you will realize that I am in my Father, and you are in me, and I am in you. Whoever has my commands and obeys them, he is the one who loves me. He who loves me will be loved by my Father, and I too will love him and show myself to him (John 14:15-21).

I realized then that to show my love for Jesus meant I had to keep His Word.

When Jesus had spoken these words, He went out with us over the Brook Kidron, where there was a garden, which we entered. He withdrew from us about a stone's throw to pray by Himself. He came later to us, but we were asleep. He said to me, "Could you men not keep watch with me for one hour? Watch and pray so that you will not fall into temptation. The spirit is willing, but the body is weak" (Matt. 26:40-41).

While He was yet speaking and with sleep still in our eyes, a multitude arrived, including Judas, who drew near to Jesus to kiss Him. When we saw what was going to happen, I said, "Lord, shall I strike with the sword?" And before He answered me, I struck the servant of the high priest, cutting off his right ear.

Jesus told me, "Put your sword back in its place…for all who draw the sword will die by the sword. Do you think I cannot call on my Father, and he will at once put at my disposal more than twelve legions of angels? But how then would the Scriptures be fulfilled that say it must happen in this way?" (Matt. 26:52-54). Again, my acting without thinking made me feel very small.

Jesus touched the servant's ear and healed him. This was the hour for the power of darkness, and I could feel it all around us. Having arrested

Jesus, the soldiers led Him and brought Him into the high priest's house. I followed at a distance.

I waited outside the courtyard. A girl at the door brought me inside and announced, "This man was with him" (Luke 22:56).

I answered, "Woman, I don't know him" (Luke 22:57).

It was cold, so the servants and guards had built a fire and were standing around it, warming themselves. I, too, felt cold and went over to warm myself. As I was standing there, they said to me, "You also are one of them" (Luke 22:58).

"Man, I am not!" (Luke 22:58).

Then one of the servants (a relative of the man whose ear had been cut off said, "Certainly this fellow was with him, for he is a Galilean" (Luke 22:59).

"Man, I don't know what you're talking about!" (Luke 22:60). At once a rooster crowed.

Who is clean? My heart failed when Jesus looked directly at me as He left the courtyard (Luke 22:61), and I ran and ran until I couldn't run anymore, so I fell on my face onto the ground, pounding my fist into the grass, kicking and throwing that dirt all over myself. I could see no good thing in me so began tearing at my cloak. I wished I had never been born. I again beat on the hard ground with my fist. Then the tears flowed like a river that had not been unleashed for ages. Cry—yes, the big fisherman cried. How long, only God knows.

My Teacher, my Master, told me before it happened, and I denied knowing Him, the One I had confessed was Jesus, the Son of God. I felt utterly devastated then felt my sword by my side. I remembered a proverb my mother would always tell me when I used cussing words. "Reckless words pierce like a sword" (Prov. 12:18). I unleashed that ungodly thing and threw it as hard as I could; cowards and deniers don't have the right to carry a sword.

Jesus, you were the reason for the hope that was inside me, a fatherless man, my hope, and I denied you. When I finally came to some sense of time, I ambled back to hide with the others, who also were afraid. Judas had killed himself, and Jesus had been crucified. Joseph of Arimathea and Nicodemus took the body and wrapped it in a clean linen cloth, just like the day the babe lay in a manger when Mary wrapped those beautiful, little feet to keep them warm and hugged Him to her bosom, singing that sweet song.

When the earth quaked and darkness descended in the middle of the day, I felt it shake my very inner soul. But now, Jesus was gone, gone from me physically, the big fisherman who couldn't even be at the foot of the cross to say I love you. Gone was a part of me, crushed beyond words. What had three years taught me? Wasn't I listening? He always included me, John, and James in most of His miracles, and we sat nights listening to His teachings. Judas, why? I couldn't throw a stone now, even at him.

John told how Jesus had hung between two other criminals and about the dividing of His garments by casting lots (John 19:18-24). The people stood looking on, sneering, saying, "He saved others...but he can't save himself!" (Mark 15:31). Later an inscription was written over Him in letters of Greek, Latin, and Hebrew: "JESUS OF NAZARETH, THE KING OF THE JEWS" (John 19:19).

We all were quiet and ate in silence, waiting until the Sabbath was over. The women had prepared some spices and talked about how they would take it to the tomb early in the morning.

Andrew and James kept comforting me by saying how Jesus always— even when I goofed up—always loved on me. He was always calling me the little rock.

Very early, the women (Mary Magdalene, Joanna, Mary, the mother of James, and Salome) left to head toward the tomb, and I could not again withhold the tears that fell from my eyes. The sinking, lost feeling inside my stomach just would not ease up.

Suddenly, the women exploded into the room all talking at once and telling of all the things that they had encountered at the tomb. I felt like their words were idle tales, and none of us believed them. But...but...then, maybe. Then I took off and ran to the tomb without stopping. Stooping down, I saw the head cloth folded together by itself. I began marveling to myself at what might have happened.

But I couldn't face Him, so I headed for my boat and pushed out from the shore.

Suddenly, there He was before me. "Yes, Peter, it is I."

When Jesus appeared to the rest of the disciples and stood in the midst of us, He said, "Peace be with you" (Luke 24:36). We were afraid, but then

He asked why we were troubled? "Why do doubts rise in your minds? Look at my hands and my feet. It is I myself! Touch me and see; a ghost does not have flesh and bones, as you see I have" (Luke 24:38-39). He asked for food; then He took it and ate it in our presence.

He then opened our understanding so that we could comprehend the Scriptures. He told us to tarry in the city of Jerusalem until we were endued with power from on High. After being led out as far as Bethany, He lifted up His hands and blessed us before He was carried up into heaven (Acts 1:9). But I am getting ahead of my story.

After I had seen Him again, I just up and told the rest I was going fishing and took off. Thomas and Nathanael of Cana, James and John, and two other of the disciples followed me. We fished all night, but Jesus didn't come out to the boat. No, not this time. We didn't catch anything and that was how my disposition and spirit felt, too—just nothing. My body was tired and smelly, and I was fishing with a heavy heart because Jesus had not addressed my denial to me. It made fishing just that—fishing.

When morning light came, we were rowing in when we heard a voice saying, "Friends, haven't you any fish?" (John 21:5).

We answered Him, "*No.*" Then we heard Him say to cast the nets on the right side of the boat, and we would find some. We did, and just as quickly as the nets hit the water, they were filled with multitudes of fish. John whom Jesus loved said to me, "It is the Lord" (John 21:7). I grabbed my garments and jumped into the sea, dressing as I went. We dragged the nets to land full of large fish, one hundred and fifty-three.

Jesus said to us, "Come and have breakfast" (John 21:12). Yet none of us dared ask Him, "Is it you?" Jesus then took the bread and blessed it and gave it to us, likewise the fish. This was the third time Jesus showed Himself to us after He was raised from the dead.

So when we had finished eating, Jesus said to me, "Simon son of John, do you truly love me more than these?"

"Yes, Lord," I said, "you know that I love you"

Jesus said, "Feed my lambs" (John 21:15). Again Jesus said, "Simon son of John, do you truly love me?"

"Yes, Lord, you know that I love you" Jesus said, "Take care of my sheep"

Now when He asked me the third time, I felt grieved inside and said, "Lord, you know all things; you know that I love you" (John 21: 16-17).

Jesus said, "Feed my sheep" (John 21:17). Then He told me how that when I was younger I had dressed myself and went to and fro and walked where I wished.

"Yes," I said, "I was pretty much on my own since I was fifteen."

I looked up into His face, then He said, "When you are old you will stretch out your hands, and someone else will dress you and lead you where you do not want to go" (John 21:18). When He finished, He said, "*Follow me*" (John 21:19).

Again when I questioned about the others, especially John, He again told me, "You must follow me" (John 21:22).

My joy was again restored. "Praise the LORD, O my soul; all my inmost being, praise his holy name" (Ps. 103:1). My heart was light for the first time in over five days. I might add that breakfast that morning on the shore was the best tasting ever.

Now back to when Jesus departed for heaven, we again felt sad. We had to have the angels tell us to quit gazing up into the heavens. He would return just like He left they told us.

Because he went up into the clouds, soon we all moved into another chapter of our lives. We would be walking this one alone, without His physical presence. We moved slowly toward Jerusalem and to the upper room, each to our own thoughts. What was coming? A Comforter?

3

Meeting, Anna

Thinking back on what I went through several years ago before leaving to follow Jesus, hearing with my heart, I remember the fishing day when I met Anna. After fishing, Andrew and I were closer to the eastern shore of the Sea of Galilee, the country of the Gadarenes near the village of Khersa or Gadara, as some called it. We docked there to sell our fish to the small village, which was in Gentile territory. The people always welcomed us because getting good fish was different than eating pork, which was their main diet. As we were loading and unloading, that's when I noticed it was her.

Slender, small in stature, with long, flowing hair, she looked just like she did when I first saw her on the west side of Galilee when she was skipping the pebbles like feathers over the waves. What was she doing here, acting casually and browsing around the fishing tables, smiling and having light conversation? Then I saw her take one of my bigger fish, called musht (meaning comb) and hide it under her cloak. She turned and headed out of town, going toward the tombs. Didn't she know about the two demon-possessed men—so exceedingly fierce so that no one could pass that way? What in the world was she thinking?

I dropped my net and started following her. What was I thinking? My big stature and all, surely she was going to figure it out, but she noticed nothing. She kept her feet heading in the direction of her heart, which had set the course, and kept that big smelly fish from falling from her arms.

As she got closer to the tombs, the roar—ungodly sounds—came, and the demon possessed men stood several yards away. She froze just where she was, standing for a moment then continued on, inching with slow, small steps up the path. I froze, too, right behind a great big boulder.

She then with that arm of hers began to twirl and twirl that fish like a towel over her head. Suddenly, she let it go just like skipping a rock with a blast of energy behind it. Splat! It landed almost perfectly in front of one of the men.

They both grabbed at the fish, and with guttural sounds and animalistic antics, they began devouring it and clawing each other. God of Abraham, what was I seeing? I turned.

Little did I know that she had turned also and was running with all her might back down the mountainside when boom— and I do mean boom—I found myself falling over and over with a frightened, little tyke of a lass tangled up with six feet of fisherman.

She was sobbing; her body and tears confirmed the heart of the matter. She pushed me aside, and without even an excuse me, apology, or I'm sorry for stealing your fish, she adjusted her feet and put more wings on them. She was gone out of my sight before I had the wits about me to even yell at her. Yell! I certainly could. I had hoped that she might have heard my loud expression of thoughts as she hurried away. Those would have made even the Sons of Thunder proud. Doesn't that blame, blame woman ever walk?

"Come on, Andrew. We're getting off this shore. I have had it."

Later in the month while waiting for the weather to improve the fishing, I saw her again. I thought, *Now what is she doing over here, this Gentile woman?* She was skipping the rocks just like she skipped the fish, just like it was a light, little piece of nothing, and each one skipped and skipped along the waves. I pondered this action again and was quite impressed, even for me.

Then she turned and seeing me took to running. As she passed me, she threw money toward me. One coin hit my forehead. *Simon, are you going to take this anymore?* was the thought that was in my brain. I decided, "No, not this athletic, big fisherman." I said to myself, "So running is your game. We shall see."

Out of breath, I finally caught her and got several smart kicks in the legs. I finally realized I was holding too tightly and let her arm go. "I'm sorry for taking your fish, you big oaf," she told me. "I know Jews don't usually talk to Samaritans, so I was waiting here for you so I could pay for the one I took," she blurted in a tone of anger as she rubbed her arm. I watched her lovely, long hair swaying back and forth as she was letting me have a piece of her mind.

"My mother and I have had to provide for ourselves since our father left us to live among the tombs. He was once a good, kind, and caring husband and a great father to me," she explained. "I can't bear to see him like this, but no one wants to go near the tombs because everyone is so afraid, especially of Legion. If your belief in a God is true, I hope you will not mind me telling you I don't believe in anything. I only see the suffering among our people because of the cruel taxation and oppression from the dictatorial Romans. And the suffering of my father. Yes, where is your God?"

From then on we met more and more, and what little knowledge I learned from Salome, I passed on to Anna. I told her about Andrew and John the Baptist. She said that she would go check this out for herself. Little did I know that she was becoming a believer but was keeping this a secret since she was part Roman and part Jew.

My big heart would pound and pound the more I saw her, and so I married her and had her mother too, live with us. I love her; she is my catch of the catch. Even Andrew agreed.

Our home became a meeting place for Jesus and His disciples. Anna and her mother love Jesus and loved having Him come to our home.

One spring morning, Andrew and Anna planned a trip to Jerusalem. Anna's mother wasn't feeling well but good enough to take care of herself. I had already left earlier in the week to be about Jesus's work.

Later that day, I bid Jesus to come and rest at my house. When we entered the house, we found Anna's mother very fevered and ill in bed. Jesus, seeing her fevered state, touched her hand, and immediately, she was made whole and arose to wait on us. By that evening, many who were sick and possessed of devils were brought to Jesus, and He healed them all. Jesus preformed many miracles in our sight. The day He rebuked the wind and the sea is the day I saw that even the things of nature like the wind and sea obey Him. I avowed that so would I.

Meanwhile, Jesus warned unbelievers, especially in Korazin and Bethsaida, that if Tyre and Sidon had seen all that was done they would have changed their lives long ago. He also warned Capernaum. The people there had seen the miracles and still refused to accept Jesus or the One who sent Him.

Now in so small a world (yes, even smaller than I thought), I was in shock when the Master said, "Let's go over to Gadarenes." It was said that Legion could be heard for miles crying in the night, and yet, Jesus headed for the town. When we arrived, the two men were coming toward the Master. The demons cried out from Legion saying, "What do you want with us, Son of God? Have you come here to torture us before the appointed time?" (Matt. 8:28-29).

At that time a large herd of swine was feeding at some distance from them. The demons begged Jesus, "If you drive us out, send us into the herd of pigs" (Matt. 8:31). He told them to go. So they came out and entered into the swine, and suddenly, the whole herd rushed down the steep bank into the sea and perished in the water. Then those who kept the herd fled. They went away into the city and told everything, including what had happened to the demon possessed men.

When the herdsmen returned, they saw the two men, one of whom was called legion sitting at Jesus's feet, clothed and in their right mind because the demons were gone. The people were still all afraid, so they asked Jesus to depart from their region.

Marcus begged to go with Jesus, but Jesus sent him away saying, "Go home to your family and tell them how much the Lord has done for you, and how he has had mercy on you." (Mark 5:19-20). Marcus went and began to proclaim in Decapolis how much Jesus had done for him, and everyone was amazed.

I pondered whether or not to tell Anna about her father. This would mean a separation because I knew that she would want to go to him. Of course, I told her, but she would have to go to Gadarenes by herself, for it was not safe for her and her mother to go together. Later, I met Anna on the lower path and told her about the miraculous healing of her father. She agreed not to mention this healing yet to her mother until she could go and prepare the way. I prearranged Anna's passage on a fishing boat, dressing her like a lad fisherman for protection. She told me of the inflammatory talk in Jerusalem ever since Jesus overturned the moneychanger's tables. I was concerned for her safety but knew that God's protection would be with her.

One day Jesus, James, John, and I went to Mount Hermon. Jesus was transfigured right before our eyes. His clothes became as white as the light, and we saw Moses and Elijah as they appeared before us talking to Jesus. We were commanded not to tell anyone about this event until after Jesus had risen from the dead.

We then headed for Jerusalem. The town of Samaria would not welcome Jesus, so James and John wanted to call fire down from heaven and destroy the people. Jesus turned and scolded them. I thought, *It's about time for those two.* As we all were walking along the road, Jesus said, "No one who puts his hand to the plow and looks back is fit for service in the kingdom of God" (Luke 9:62). It seemed to me as time went on that His instructions and teachings increased in depth. He taught many things such as obey the teaching of God and happiness comes, be a light for the world, don't be like the Pharisees, don't act selfishly, don't worry excessively, don't put your trust in money, remember to pray as He taught (Our Father in Heaven, hallowed be your name, Matt. 6:9), and remember that God's kingdom is within you.

He told us that we must accept the kingdom of God as a little child would, or we would never enter it. The kingdom of heaven is like a net that was put into the lake and caught many different kinds of fish. When the net was full, the fishermen pulled it to the shore. They sat down and put all the good fish in baskets and threw away the bad fish. It will be this way at the end of the world. The angels will come and separate the evil people from the good people. The angels will throw the evil people into the blazing furnace, where the people will cry and grind their teeth in pain. The good, however, will go to their reward in heaven. We enjoyed those times when Jesus would stop at Mary and Martha's home. We could breathe a sigh and relax. My thoughts would go to Anna— Anna, what are you doing now? Goodnight, Anna.

4

Anna and Her Father

The boat was a fishing vessel, but I didn't care. I had to get to the other side of the Sea of Galilee. Thanks to Simon's friends, I got the ride for free. It was more than a miracle. When Peter came home, he told me what Jesus had done, delivering my father and Legion from the prison of those tombs.

The waves were a little high, but I love this old sea and enjoyed the ride as my heart was racing inside, and my thoughts were many. Will he recognize me? Will he remember all that went on with the days and nights of terror and hell on earth?

I ran up the hill that was so familiar to me when a child. It was easy to find him. Everyone was begging to hear the story of what happened, and he kept telling it as long as there was one to listen. "Father, it's me, Anna."

"Anna? No, am I to be blessed again, oh daughter. You have grown so and are as lovely as your mother."

"Let's go, Father. Where are you staying? Father, do you know how dangerous the situation is with the Jews and all the trouble in Jerusalem?" We talked way into the night. He asked about Mother, how we survived when he left, and how Simon came into my life. "Yes, Father, I stole his fish, and then I knocked him down. Of course, I later paid for it, but that was the beginning. You might say you brought us together. How's that for a story?"

The next morning my father looked at me and asked, "Anna, aren't you feeling well?" "No, Father, I feel I might be getting what mother had before I left." That afternoon there was a knock at the door. Marcus had come to see Father, but when he saw me, he said he had a remedy that might help my illness.

As the days went by, Father looked after me tenderly. When Marcus returned, Father told him, "Thanks, Marcus, that medicine is helping. I have forgotten how many days it has been, but today Anna asked for some tea and that may be a good sign."

"Well, if you need me, just head for Decapolis. I will be telling those people about what Jesus did for me. Right! He did it for us both."

I looked at the sky, the hot tea feeling good on my throat. To think it was my loving father that brought me through my illness. How long is long when you are ill. Months had now passed, and in town people were talking about the zealots and the uprising among the Jews. We were also hearing noise about a locust-eating man being beheaded. "Oh, John, how could they?" Now fear was really at its height.

Then one afternoon, some soldiers marched into the city, laughing and drinking and bragging about the capture of Jesus. Father could not believe how they could do this. Just look at what Jesus had done in his life! He had been demon possessed, and Jesus had set him free. Could they not see that this Man was different?

"Father, come away from the window. Please, we must keep ourselves as safe as we can by keeping a low profile. Yes, I know you love talking about the Man of Galilee, and how He gave you and us another chance at living."

"But, Anna, don't you hear what they are saying? The city of Magdala has been burned to the ground."

"Yes, they were looking for Jesus at Mary Magdalene's home, and they found Barabbas in the city. Father, Mother was feeling ill the day I left. I am wondering if she survived and if poor, darling Simon and Andrew took care of her?" I went over and hugged him and said, "I love you for nursing me back to wellness, and every day I feel I'm getting stronger."

"Oh, the God of father Abraham, I pray that my Simon is safe."

Father began to sink more into himself. He now was going to his room and skipping supper. "Father, come and eat your supper? What? You're not hungry? Father, you know how much Mom and I love you, and when this trouble dies down, it will be safe again to travel. We will go back to where Simon and I live, to my lovely home in Capernaum." Again and again, I reassured my father of my love and that I too did not understand what was happening to all of us. I told my father about John the Baptist, about our fishing boats, about Salome and her two sons, James and John, and about life in Capernaum.

"Yes, Father, I love you and am so glad we are now believers. "Please Jesus, remember us Gentiles," I whispered in silence.

"Mother said she would come, but with the roads and villages all under curfew, Roman soldiers are everywhere. I know she can't come now."

"Oh, the God of father Abraham, I pray that my big fisherman is still alive, and he, too, has not been beheaded."

"Father, Jesus changed Simon's name to Peter. It was hard for me to call him this, so I usually said, 'Simon Peter Barjona,' especially when I wanted to get him to listen. How I love that big fisherman. He would toss me up in the air so effortlessly and giggle with the biggest voice he had and then say with a grin, 'Would I ever let any harm come to my little turtle dove?' He said some more things, I believe from Solomon's writings. He then patted the sword on his side. He started carrying that weapon when he joined the group that traveled with Jesus."

"Oh the God of father Abraham, I pray he will never have to resort to using it; however, I know that wild animals are around, especially at night, and it will protect him from them. I pray that within his soul my fisherman knows that there has to be a reason I am not at his side and haven't returned home with Father. Gentiles and Jews are not a good mix right now, anyway. Now even more so since many are all in arms about hearing that Jesus is a King and fearing that He is going to overthrow the 'Roman rule.'"

The noise and commotions from the street drew us to the window. "What in the world are they rejoicing about?" remarked Father.

"It sounds like they are rejoicing and chanting that Barabbas has been set free."

Grief stricken and weak, Father leaned on my arm and said, "Anna, oh, Anna." Then he began telling me about when Barabbas was growing up. "They called him 'Ab' then. His father often beat him for disobedience. Ab would sneak out at night and run after a band of hoodlums. He would throw stones and play with sticks, pretending to be one of them. He was a restless child and a grief to his mother and father.

"As he grew older, he began using slingshots and tormenting animals. He just did it for fun and amusement. One day a rock put out the eye of the goat. The goat, which was frightened, was kicking and jumping and headed for the washing tub, knocking it over. His mother jumped out of harm's way just in time as hot water and soap went everywhere. "The goat, still frightened and hurting, kicked and knocked over the make-shift chicken coop; eggs and chickens were trampled because the goat could not see. Ab laughed and said, "Bet some of those chickens are still running." He didn't care how close his mother came to being scalded. He didn't care that she would have to go carry the water again and rewash all the clothes, this time without soap as they were poor. The eggs and chickens for food were also gone. Ab didn't seem to love anything or anyone, not even his mother. He didn't care that the goat would be forever blind; the very goat that provided him milk for survival.

"He advanced to knives and then swords. He never seemed to be sorry or show remorse; even the beatings and the soft corrections were lost on his emotional soul. He toughened up his emotions, which also toughened up his heart.

"One day he went volatile hitting his father and ran. Later, we learned he had joined up with that band of no-gooders. He became one of their leaders, and once on a raid, a person was murdered.

"How could they release him over Jesus? Anna, Anna, Jesus touched my life. Ab was one reason I went mad. He and his bunch of zealots killed my brother, your uncle. He told me he would do the same to you and your mother if I turned him in. He also demanded money, as well. He is a Belial. He is utterly the opposite of Jesus. Jesus looked me right in the eyes and with a voice so soft said, 'Demons leave.' I felt His tender, compassionate love. Release Ab—how could they?"

The noise from the street grew louder. Now the chanters were shouting, "The King of the Jews has been crucified." My father pushed me away and fell on his knees. I turned and ran from the room. I ran from the house. My heartache was too heavy, and not knowing about Simon was unspeakable distress to my very own soul. Father will mourn for us both.

I ran toward the seashore under the solemn, eerie blackness adrift overhead thinking, "I must get some air. I must remember how Simon and I met. I will think of his laughter and his roughhousing with James and John. I will skip some rocks; that will calm my quaking body."

Three days later, Father still wouldn't eat. He just cried and cried. I wanted to get hold of myself, so out toward the sea I headed again. I walked again down the path toward the place that always calmed me. Finally, the sunshine once again began to break over the sea, giving it a beauty all its own. The boats were not in nor were the town people up and about. The birds in the air began circling and riding on the wind drifts above the sea. The smell of the flowers along the pathway was aloft in the air, while the yellow of the mustard seed bushes was full and swaying in the breeze.

The earthquake had been felt here, but nobody understood the meaning. Neither did they understand the three hours of darkness, which fell over the land, but underneath they knew that it had something to do with that Man that had visited them months ago when all those pigs were killed. Yes, the fear was still here, and now this silence was even worse. "Oh, Simon, I need you. We once said and agreed that the kingdom is what we wanted for all our kin and for ourselves. It's a place where peace and love will reign forever, like Andrew always repeated. We know from Jesus's teaching no one who begins to plow can keep looking back." I sighed and noticed that the ducks and herons and the other birds were going on with what they knew how to do. I thought, *I must, too.*

Turning up the path toward the cottage, I sang a little Jewish tune that Salome had taught me. My eyes caught sight of the oleander bush with its beautiful white and pink blossoms. I plucked the white one and remembered something about a folklore that the oleander flower turns white when an angel passes by. Is this why I feel so light hearted? "Father, lie down for a while. You are feeling warm. Oh, Father, please just a little water. Just a sip, please."

"Oh, Mother, I wish you were here." I whispered a prayer to the God of Simon. "May your God not forget me. Let the God of Heaven and earth keep you safe, and may I soon be home. I miss you so. May Ab's stony heart change. Mine did. John the Baptist said, 'All men can repent and be saved.'"

Days, weeks, or was it just a day. I was suffering from lack of sleep, but Father was no better. I stepped outside for a while, and when I returned to the cottage, the rooms were silent. He had the fever, but his heart would not take the abuse.

"Marcus, you have been a good friend and a great help. I appreciate the clean clothing and the supplies. I agree we must burn everything. Yes, this fever mustn't spread."

I sat down by the seashore once again and lay down with a prayer on my lips. I finally let the tears drop into the sea and asked, "Now what?"

I saw Marcus coming down the path; he was running and yelling, "We are going to Capernaum."

The crossing was great, and life again filled my loins. The love for the west side of the Sea of Galilee was just as strong as it was on the east.

"Mother, where are you?" I yelled, running straight through the unlocked door of the house. I searched the whole house. Only silence greeted me here. "Oh, God of Abraham, please help!"

We then ran to the house of Zebedee. "Oh, it is so good to see you." I fell on their necks and wept for joy. "Yes, yes, please fill us in on all that has happened."

Slowly the months were unfolded to me. I wept and wept. My beloved fisherman was alive and was with my mother in Jerusalem.

"We must go now," said Salome. I was being hurried to prepare for leaving again, but this time it will be toward Jerusalem to an upper room to tarry. Risen, He is risen is still ringing in my ears. Simon Peter must explain all this to me. He must!

5

Upper Room, Welcome Home

The days were long, but we waited like Jesus told us, 120 in the upper room in Jerusalem. We talked about His teachings and rejoiced about His being alive and rising from the grave, the future for all mankind and for us, the beginning of a body, which would soon become known as Christians. Jesus promised eternal life and a kingdom that is to come, where He will be our King, the Lion of Judah, who will sit upon the throne of David forever.

We broke bread, slept, and prayed. We let the mother of Jesus tell us about when He was a little boy, about the time Jesus stayed at the temple when He said He was about His Father's business. Now we knew more than ever that He did His Father's will and was truly the Emmanuel sent from God.

We knew that we were called to be witnesses of His resurrection, birthed into a living hope of Jesus Christ when He was raised from the dead and into an inheritance that is imperishable, undefiled, and unfading, kept in heaven for us.

Suddenly, the wind blew as of a mighty, rushing force, and it filled the whole house where we were sitting. Then there appeared on us divided tongues as of fire that sat upon each of our heads. We were seen as drunken men and women.

We began speaking in a heavenly language (later called speaking in tongues), but everyone heard the Good News in his or her own language. The Gospel of the Good News will now begin.

I can only tell you that my spirit was moved by the Holy Spirit. Afraid— no, not this big fisherman. This time everyone will hear me out about the God of Abraham, Isaac, and Jacob. They will hear how Jesus, the Christ, the Son of God, was crucified and arose three days later, conquering death, hell, and the grave.

Yes, three thousand repented and were baptized that same day. Awe came upon everyone after that because of the wonders and signs being done. For example, John and I told the cripple at the temple, "Silver or gold I do not have, but what I have I give you. In the name of Jesus Christ of Nazareth, walk" (Acts 3:6). The boldness was from my Jesus, and this was a witness to my spirit that He truly was still with me though I could not see Him in the physical.

Pages couldn't hold all that went on from that day. Many people began believing. However, others, including most of the high officials, did not believe but began adding to the persecution. Yes, persecution had begun, many spending days and nights in prison. One night the angel delivered me out to and through the gates of the prison. I first thought it was a dream, but it was real. The authorities beheaded our beloved James, and I would have been next except for the intervention of God's hand.

The floggings increased and orders were given not to speak in His name; however, we did not cease to teach and proclaim Jesus as the Messiah. Remembering what our Lord did gave us courage.

I cried over Stephen. That day a severe persecution began against the whole church in Jerusalem, so we began to scatter throughout Judea and Samaria. We began to hold services secretly. Saul was ravaging against us even to entering house after house, dragging men and women off to prison. Someday, I shall see Saul face-to-face.

Philip was strong for the Lord and was tuned into hearing what the Holy Spirit wanted for him. He went around preaching the Word to the city of Samaria, and they, seeing the signs and healings, accepted the Word of God with great joy in that city.

John and I went down to pray for them and laid hands on them so that they might receive the Holy Spirit. One man there offered me money to buy this power. However, this gift cannot be obtained with money.

Philip took the message to the Ethiopian eunuch. He proclaimed the Good News to all the towns until he came to Caesarea. Meanwhile, I did not know that God was dealing with Saul.

I went here and there among all the believers and then went to Lydia. Aeneas had been bedridden for eight years, but God healed him. In Joppa, Dorcas was brought back from the dead. In Caesarea, Cornelius and his whole household came into the faith, and we knew then that God shows no partiality, but that in every nation anyone who fears Him and does what is right is accepted. Yes, God has given to the Gentiles the repentance that leads to life.

The day Herod Agrippa had James killed with the sword triggered the memory of my sword. Little did I know that Andrew would also suffer so much. He too would die. I heard that a Roman woman took his body down and buried him. The cross he endured was in the shape of an X. He loved the Lord to his end.

Barnabas and Saul were in the church in Antioch, where the Holy Spirit commissioned them for the work that they should do, and after fasting and praying, they were sent out with God's blessing. I heard the reports that Saul's name was changed to Paul. Then reports came of Paul and Barnabas in Seleucia and Cyprus. They also went to Antioch of Pisidia and Iconium, then to Lystra and Derbe. Finally, they came to Jerusalem and talked to the elders and the apostles about what had happened and about all the signs and wonders that God had done through them among the Gentiles.

Paul and Silas set out to Derbe and to Lystra to instruct the young man Timothy, as churches were strengthened in the faith and increased in numbers daily. I then heard of Paul's arrest and his being transported to Rome.

I look around my prison cell. Yes, I was glad I had written those two letters (first and second Peter) to Christians, God's chosen people, to people who have been uprooted and scattered away from their home and loved ones. Yes, I was glad that I could, in my last minutes on earth, believe that as they read the letters they will hold on to the living hope. Yes, I know about failure and doing things because I did not understand. I wrote that they should become as obedient servants, and I encouraged them to do this and fight the good fight of faith. I was glad for the church in Babylon and sent them encouragement to stand strong in God's grace, knowing that someday God will make everything right.

God keeps us from falling, and we share a glory that will continue forever. I reminded the elders to watch over God's flock.

My youth spent with the sheep and fishing is where God began to look after me. I remember then, as well, that it was an angel that watched over me and caused me to dream of love and peace. "It took a while, Andrew, but I, the big fisherman, have finally gotten it. God is a good God."

My thoughts were jarred back to reality as the sounds of the iron gates being opened broke into the silence. I thought, *What, no, I'm not going easily. My arms are still strong.* Then something hit my spirit and thoughts: "Someone else will dress you and lead you where you do not want to go (John 21:18). "Peter, do you love me" (John 21:17)

I stopped struggling. I said with the best courage a big, old fisherman has, "Then hang me upside down…Lord, I do love you." I began to whisper, "Our Father in heaven, hallowed be your name…" (Matt. 9:6).

Slowly, as the pressure hit his brain and eardrums, he heard back in Bethlehem Mary's singing to the babe "foxes have holes and birds have nest." But…then another vision burst forth. It was of Anna, running and skipping pebbles into the sea. As it faded, he heard, "Yes, Peter, you do love Me. Welcome home my good and faithful servant."

"Guard, did you see that light around Peter's feet?"

"Yes, and it appears to be like a star beam. I can't tell you what that's about Gaius, but I think I am beginning to believe in what he preached."

"Gaius, there are three people here to take the body. One is Anna, his wife. She is with two men, John Mark and Marcus."

As Anna, Marcus, and John Mark gaze on Peter's scarred, marred body, Anna turns to John Mark and says, "John, I know how much Peter loved you, and I want to thank you for being a spiritual son to him. It meant so much to him to have you travel with him and assist with the letters he wrote." As he shrouded Peter's face, John Mark tenderly wiped away a tear that lingered on Peter's cheek.

"Sleep on, Simon, my beloved, you have earned your crown," wept Anna as she held him one more time. "One day we'll be together again, so until then…I leave Rome with two thoughts. One question is for the people on earth, 'Are you prepared for His kingdom?'

"The second is for little star beam, 'Can you take us all safely back to Jerusalem?'" "Yes, look North, it's me!"

6

Rome: John Mark

Afraid of the persecutions that were now real in Rome, where freedom of religion could not be expressed with like believers, John Mark hurried to get the wagon ready to carry Peter's body back to the Brown Door, the catacombs, the secret place for all that were believers. Now, it would become the final resting place for the beloved disciple, father, and man of faith.

The fledgling Christian community came together as a group in church service settings whenever they could. They had been blessed with many visits from Peter, as well as Andrew, Pricilla, and Aquila, Paul, and many other traveling saints. From the bottom of his heart, Peter liked to lead the singing even though sometimes out of key. When they all came together in worship, he would let the Spirit lead him, and the Spirit blessed him over and over.

Sometimes this would cause everyone to shout enthusiastically and to dance with joy. The mouth that once denied the King of kings and Lord of lords would praise and worship the One who forgave and restored him to a life worth living. The faith that the worshipers received through Peter's encouragement and his singing gave them the desire to live another day even if the result was death.

Yes, worshippers had to meet in secret, which was not always easy. They lived in fear that the soldiers would come and take Peter away and take the rest of them to the arena for Nero's fun and games. Many became discouraged because of fear. However, they soon felt His (Jesus Christ) faith replace their fear. They began to enjoy praising Him and witnessed healings again and again. Sometimes they fasted and came into agreement with the Spirit using the words of the Torah, praying without ceasing for loved ones, for the city of Rome, and for Christians in Antioch.

The catacombs, where Christians had to hide in secret, were now chosen by Anna for the final resting place for her loving husband, her Simon. John Mark, Anna, and Petronilla quietly rode in welcome silence, returning this time with Peter's body. Yet, in sorrow they knew that he had died, loving and strong, with his faith in the One who asked him, "Peter, do you love me?"

Still in mourning for his beloved friend, John Mark went to find travel passage for the three of them. He finally found passage heading toward Rhegium and then on to Fair Haven. Their final destination would be Joppa, just thirty-three miles from Jerusalem, where John Mark's sweet mother lived. God bless her soul, she had always held him up in prayer for God's will to be accomplished in his life.

Heading back to the Brown Door, John Mark passed a vegetable and fruit stand. Fruit always reminded him of the fruit markets in Jerusalem, and he couldn't resist purchasing some. Little did he know that taking a few moments to buy a small bag of fruit would be the miracle that would protect his life.

Upon John Mark's entrance to the secret place, he was greeted with silence. "What has happened?" John Mark proclaimed. The tables were upturned, the basins were broken, and the chairs were all in disarray. No one was there, so what happened to Peter's body? "No! No!" he cried. Turning, he quickly knew he had to hide, so he fled down to the pier to hide for the rest of the night. At all cost, he must protect Peter's writings, "The Good News." The Good News must be proclaimed according to Jesus's last command before He went to heaven.

Throughout the long night, John Mark kept a lookout for Roman guards, asking questions about any Christians or traveling people. "Anna, precious Anna and Petronilla. Oh, Petronilla, only I know how I am starting to fall in love with you," John Mark mused. However, John Mark knew where his strength lay, so he prayed, "God, be gracious and forget them never. Please keep them safe."

The next morning at early light, John Mark boarded a cargo ship. He said to the captain, "Can you use another hearty sailor with a strong back? I'll work out the wages for my fare, Captain, sir." The captain agreed and pointed to a barrel filled with rum and then to the hatchway, which went to the lower level. Reaching the bowels of the ship, John Mark took the barrel to the stern and set it alongside the others that were already loaded. He then noticed a strong smell of cheese mixed with grain along with the odor of old ship boards. He slipped the pouch with "The Good News" papers behind a barrel before leaving.

Underneath John Mark's sense of "I know it all" composure, he strongly desired that this vessel was up and sailing, saying to himself, "Let's be outward bound, now!" Thinking back to his younger days, he was very thankful he had tagged along with his father when he visited the ships in port to assist the captains with their paperwork. While there, John Mark was free to play and run. He silently thanked his father for letting him on board when he handled the sales of the merchandise going here and there. "At least", he thought, "I learned some of the information on chores that needed to be done while running a vessel even though I had to be among the riff- raft and other ruffians and often got in their way." Sometimes, they would express their anger with explicit remarks.

Thinking about verbal trouble, John Mark remembered when met with that kind of trouble after sailing with Paul and Barnabas. *Alas*, he thought, *but I can't think about what happened in the past right now. I've got to heave that rum keg like I have done it all my life.*

John Mark watched the process for a minute then heard someone yelling for one of the sailors, calling him Mugface. John Mark quickly made a decision and stepped into action. This was a man to have as a friend rather than a foe. "Here, Mugface, let me have that grog, and you take the other." Mugface half-grinned, and that was the welcome John Mark wanted. This weathered sailor didn't want to look like he couldn't handle the bigger grog barrel, so John Mark took it, leaving the smaller one for Mugface.

Finally, the captain yelled out another order, "Lower the stern line and get those spring lines." Yes, soon they were outward bound, heading for the open sea.

"Whew! Thank God I am now on board and working with the men. This will be a good decoy for me instead of having the appearance of just being a paying traveler. Hurry, please set the larger sails," he whispered in constant prayer, as he messed up his hair and tunic and hurried back up onto the deck to get more cargo.

Later, in the quiet of the voyage, John Mark wondered if anyone escaped from the raid on the Brown Door. "God, please keep them safe," he prayed. "Maybe my friends took Peter's body somewhere else and hid themselves with it."

John Mark decided to wait until most of the crew retired for the night to retrace his steps and pick up the hidden pouch. He would bring it back to the cabin to hide in a safe place. So instead of heading toward Mugface's cabin to bunk down, he moved quietly, around rustic pillars and down steps toward the cargo of grog barrels where he had earlier slipped the pouch. Searching for a few minutes-finally- he felt the hidden pouch -pulled it out over the barrels and hugged it to him.

Safety for Peter's letter holding truth for the Christian family was now stronger than ever. John Mark's admiration for Peter and Jesus and his Disciples, has grown since he was twelve. All of them met in his family home in Jerusalem, homesick a little now thinking about Peter- but those twelve men they all had different talents and personalities. John Mark wondered how Jesus knew them so well, until Peter told him that Jesus had gone off by himself and prayed to His Father all night before choosing the ones that would become apostles. John Mark remembered watching how Jesus, at certain times, only had to look at them, and they would straighten up their act. *Yes,* John Mark thought, *I think I will write how quickly they all responded when Jesus would speak.* At other times, however, they seemed not to understand at all. Yes, the healings, the miracles, Jesus would speak, and what He said happened. "I must make sure that Christians understand this about Jesus." Yes, he felt he must write this all down.

Jesus always had a moment for him. Even as a young child, John Mark never felt that his questions bothered the Lord. Jesus spoke to John Mark about His own youth and schooling. He remarked about being obedient in all things that were on God's heart. He said He was here on earth to do His Father's will. He encouraged John Mark to study the Torah with great enthusiasm. He told John Mark that His Father loved the world and everyone in it. He loved everything, from every minute particle within the atom to the farthest galaxy, both in the spiritual realm and the physical. There is nothing too small or too great that is beyond God's sphere of influence and God's love for His creation.

Uncle Barnabas, Matthew, Andrew, James, John, and Peter were frequent guests at John Mark's home in Jerusalem. His mother loved having the group and spared no expense to welcome them all, giving them lots of love and hospitality for their time in her home. Peter was John Mark's favorite, becoming like a big brother to him. John Mark loved Peter's hearty laugh. They would arm wrestle at times with Peter showing John Mark who the boss was, so to speak. The relationship between Peter and John Mark continued to grow with the years, but now Peter was dead. "Time, ahh, each of us has been given our measure of time, and it slips away day by day. We never know how much time we have been given," he pondered.

John Mark missed his own father also, who because of his business was in Libya more than he was in Jerusalem. Their family left Cyrene because of the attacks of the Berbers, who were nomadic pastoral people wanting more land. John Mark's mother felt that they would be safer in Jerusalem, and she wanted her children to be raised in the Jewish faith. They brought their household servants with them, little Rhoda who was like a sister and her mother. Rhoda quickly learned how prayer was answered when Christians gathered in John Mark's home prayed for Peter's release from jail, not wanting him to be killed like James. Peter scared her when he was at the door waiting to be let in. She thought that he was a ghost. John Mark smiled at that memory.

The family all felt better after the move; however, since the influence of Greek philosophy had begun spreading over the area, Cyrene became the artistic center for the Greek world. John Mark's father continued to conduct business with Cyrene and Alexandria, which demanded more of his time and constant trips back and forth.

One fateful night while on the dock inspecting, pricing, and cataloguing the barrels awaiting shipment, John Mark's father was ambushed and killed by a band of thieves. It was hard to take the news. After his father's death, however, the disciples, especially Peter, became John Mark's role models.

Jesus was taken from John Mark, too. He never would forget that horrible night in the Garden! Tears and cries break forth from his mother and the other women. Then Peter and all the disciples went into hiding—all were afraid. John Mark remembered his embarrassment and the shame and anger he felt toward those that took the Master.

Because of his current situation and the fear that was upon him, John Mark knew that he had to pray now. One positive and strong example he had learned from his mother and the disciples—prayer changes things when your faith resides in Him. He got down on his knees and began, "Our Father, which art in heaven…"

After praying, John Mark leaned now his back against a bigger barrel and thought about the pouch he was holding. He came to the conclusion that it might be safer in a different location than taking it back to the cabin, deciding the old man might decide to snoop. *Yes, I will take it further back in the ship and hide it behind the household goods. Then I can retrieve it when we reach the Port of Rhegium,* he sleepily thought.

Exhausted from the previous sleepless night and the hard toil of a sailor's work, before long John Mark, holding the pouch, embraced the quiet rhythm of the waves and, like a baby in a swing, was soon fast asleep.

Mugface in His Cabin

"Come here, Etan," called Mugface. "Soon we will be in old Rhegium, a friendly port if ever there was one. I feel like I want to go visit our favorite tavern and my old friends. Maybe I'll take along that young sailor I just met."

Etan, the cat, strong and impetuous, enjoyed his master stroking him over and over again as he was lifted from the small box into awaiting arms. Mug used the small box as a chair, a table, and a step stool. It also had a little hole behind it, which was the perfect spot for his grog money. He walked over to the box and pulled out the wadded stash he would need to go wenching tonight.

"Now where is that young one? The one that's trying to be a rough and tough sailor lad. Hee hee", Mugface said, grinning at Etan. Etan was meowing now and wanting something more than a few strong strokes. "Here Etan, let me get those fish heads from the galley for you. Now be patient; after all, you're supposed to catch your own akhbars. Remember, that was the deal with our dear ole Captain."

Etan carried a big part of the fish head toward the dingy, dirty corner near the back of the bunk when Mugface noticed something in the corner. *Now what's that in the corner,* he thought, as he got closer to investigate. Walking through the dimly lit room, he was startled to say the least and shouted, "It's another beast."

Well, shocked, shocked was the word all right when Mugface found another cat he didn't need. "So you're a stowaway—huh?" Now what was he to do with a mother cat who lost her kittens? He looked at Etan with that "Don't look back at me like you don't know this is all your doing from our last stop in port, you pirate!"

"You old faithless beggar. Ye were always a wild one."

Mug remembered when he first saw Etan. The cat had followed him around until Mug finally grew so attached to him that he hid him under his coat and took Etan back to the ship. Mugface took a beating for that little stunt. He remembered being sore and stiff for days. "You ungrateful creature, you." Mugface growled.

Mugface decided he needed to name this feline since she was going to be around for a while. "Let's just call you Kato." Kato looked up, following Mug's movement with her eyes; then suddenly, she leaped toward the corner, hissing and extending her claws. "So little stowaway, you look terrible and look like you haven't eaten for a while." With Etan and Kato on board this old rig of a ship, it will be slim pickings from the galley. Mugface just shook his head and told Kato she would have to work for her dinner just like Etan and eliminate some of those akhbars like the Captain demanded. Taking his calloused, rough hand with the two missing fingers, he picked Kato up and began to stroke her head. He felt the fear leave and a contented purring began to fill the room.

"So, Etan, my pet, lover boy of the Mediterranean Sea, now what do we do now?" Mugface inquired. He noticed that Etan was already showing his helpfulness. Etan had pushed his fish head toward the scared little female with a big white diamond mark on her forehead. Mugface figured that wild one was smitten even for an old cat. Etan exited the dim, dingy room, knowing it was an akhbar dinner for him tonight if he wanted anything to eat since his portion of fish was given to Kato. He dashed toward the crack under the old, rough, ragged door of Mugface's cabin and headed toward the stern of the ship.

Yes, she has a perfect diamond marking, if I do say so myself, thought Mug watching Kato who was now back meowing for more food after enjoying everything on the floor, but all the fish heads were gone. "Sorry, me lady, but that's all there is." Finding an old patch blanket, he snuggled it around Kato, and soon from exhaustion, she began purring and accepted the peace of sleep.

Etan

John Mark was aware that rats boarded all ships that docked side by side at the pier. The akhbars could easily climb up the spring lines onto the boat and then get to the cargo, which was sometimes grain and boxed cheeses. The smell alone would bring them in by the dozens. He had carried a piece of wood with him to protect himself on his journey through the ship; however, it now benignly lay beside him as he slept. While sleeping, unbeknownst to him, many tiny eyes scrutinized his sleeping form—eyes that belonged to several akhbars that huddled in small inconspicuous spaces, waiting—just waiting to get to the cargo this night.

Etan knew these critters and how they worked, so he ran the well-known route to search out those vermin. They liked teasing him and running to hide in small spaces or cracks in the old ship's hull. Etan soon learned how to outfox them and usually ended up with a good dinner for himself. But something was different this night. He wondered about the strange feeling that lingered in the dark, night air. He didn't know why, but he was feeling an urgency to go to the lower level of the ship and make his way toward the stern. "Maybe those vermin found the larder of grain? Maybe it's just my inner cat radar," he mused.

Etan had that strong cat nature; after all, the meaning of his name is "strong," and he was a mate of Mugface who is the toughest man alive. Mugface even survived a shark attack. Yes, he is steel and gentle all rolled into one. "He took the cat-o-nine tails for me, once. Yes, he is different just like me, one-eyed, but it's better than two, sometimes."

This new female in Etan's life, Kato, was stranded from an Athenian ship, which had docked earlier at the pier. She had left the boat to get some extra food for her family, and upon her return, Kato had found that her ship had left port. She recognized that Etan knew his way around as soon as she spied him on the docks. Perhaps, she thought, if she hitched a ride with him, she just might catch up with her old ship—and her brood of kittens! She immediately followed him right up the gangplank and bravely tracked behind him as if she had done this kind of thing all her life, and as if she was supposed to be on Etan's ship.

Kato was born on a ship in Piraeus, a port near the urban area of Athens, and had spent the majority of her life onboard the Athenian ship.

She knew how to take charge very well, and now all the fish heads were hers. *I need to let her have this food and go take care of finding more food for myself,* thought Etan. *Kato's hunger must mean that she still thought she would be reunited with her kittens, so she needed to keep up her milk supply.*

The night was still feeling creepy, and Etan's hair was beginning to stand on end. He sensed that the vermin were very near. He thought they would soon be here especially if they smelled something good in the stern of the boat. Akhbars would even enjoy the grog they found in empty kegs.

Etan's inner sense intensified as he moved like a cat in the jungle, sliding on his belly and then crouching and sliding again. "There they are!" he whispered to himself. "Why are there so many, and what are they planning for dinner with such a large group?" he wondered.

Etan looked around at his surroundings and saw a young man asleep, his head lying on a leather pouch. The pouch was glowing with a dim light. It seemed like the young man's head was encircled with a crown of light. His sleep was very deep and peaceful.

How long before these vermin make their attack? Etan thought. *How can I stop this? I'll have to move when their leader, the big, ugly, black one, makes his move.* Slowly a big, black rat crept toward the calf of the young man's right leg. Etan knew what he would do if that was Mugface lying there. As he looked at the glowing pouch, Etan began to feel an inner strength and braveness like never before, and he knew what he had to do.

The battle was not pleasant for Etan, and no one came to his rescue. John Mark slept through the attack in peaceful solemnity. All Etan remembered of the battle was the pouch with the secret glow emanating from it.

John Mark

Awaking, John Mark looked around barrels at the carnage in the room. What a mess! On the port side, he saw blood and dead rats mixed together like nothing he had ever seen before. What had happened? Whatever it was, it had not attacked him. Did the God of Abraham protect him? Did Jesus?

Getting up and stepping over the mess that surrounded him, he saw, lying in front of the door leading out toward the stairs, a mangled ball of fur. Approaching very carefully, he grabbed the stick of wood to touch it. "Oh no, it is Etan, Mug's cat." John Mark quickly threw his pouch over his shoulder, picked up the cat with his tunic blouse and hurried to the small, dingy cabin in search of Mugface.

He entered the dimly lit room to find Mugface getting ready to start his day. Words were not spoken as John Mark laid down his bloody tunic. No life appeared from within, only a soggy ball of fur. Mug took one look and knew it was Etan. He went down on his knees and tried to wipe away the mess from Etan's face. Without a word, without an expression, without a wail, Mugface turned and left the room, leaving John Mark alone looking down upon the scruffy cat. Then John Mark realized that this cat had fought off the akhbar and saved his life. God had used this animal to preserve him and the writings of Peter.

John Mark removed the dishes and dirty rags from off the top of the utilitarian box and gently laid the pouch on it. Then he reached down and picked up his bloody tunic with Etan inside and tenderly laid him on top of the pouch. He remembered how Jesus had healed the man with the withered hand on the Sabbath, a miracle, and a miracle was needed now. "Please, dear Jesus, please, for Mugface's sake."

The relevant question this day would be, "Would John Mark see a miracle?" Jesus healed many, restoring sight to the blind, hearing to the deaf, and strength to the lame. "Faith, yes, faith is what I need now." John Mark sighed and left the room.

Kato came out of hiding and observed Etan and the tunic blouse lying on the box. Will Kato witness a miracle today? Will God who created all animals heal one of His creatures? Will Kato be reunited with her kittens? A miracle would encourage her even though an animal. Her milk was waning. She needed to be with her babies. She then left the room to seek some food for herself.

On Deck

Routine chores of the day were already taking place, so Mugface and John Mark took their positions pulling on the heavy canvas. Stretching it, then pulling, stretching it out again, and then pulling it tight once more. The sweat was obvious for this type of labor and so was the long sad face on Mug. His countenance was down, and he was so quiet that it made John Mark uncomfortable. John Mark wanted to move to another location, and so he did, to help out on the other side of the ship.

John Mark felt sad himself. "Why had he not awakened and come to Etan's rescue? He had carried a big enough board for protection. So many questions. Why didn't he go back to his 'bed hammock' in Mugface's room? How could he have slept through that whole ordeal? Was it something to do with the pouch?"

"Jesus, my Master and Savior, please help me and protect me in this crisis," John Mark prayed. "If these sailors should find out that I am a Jew, I would be shark bait for sure." John Mark was glad when the shout came that it was time for some food, water, and a break. This kind of labor was taking its toll on him. He noticed one crew member wrapping his stomach to help keep his muscles from being overly strained when pulling on the heavy sails. He quickly looked around the deck to see where Mugface might be taking his break and how he was doing.

"Where is Mugface anyway?" He looked over the deck again and then slipped away into the hatchway, then on toward the small hole in the ship that Mugface called his cabin. John Mark wondered what he would find. He approached the cabin slowly and heard sobbing—low sounds, but definitely sobbing. Then he heard what sounded like words of affection. "Is he mourning?" As John Mark slowly entered the room, he couldn't believe his eyes. With eyes as big as saucers, Mugface was sitting on the floor beside the box. Etan was alive and sitting up licking Mug's face. Etan was completely restored and with two good eyes. The gnaw marks from the rat attack were totally healed and his fur was like a new born kitten's. What a sight to behold!

John Mark immediately felt the Holy Spirit, and goose bumps arose all over him. He joined Mug on the floor and sat as close to the box and the pouch as he could. Kato jumped up on the box and started licking Etan. Wow, what a picture. John Mark then hugged Mugface and slipped the pouch out from under Etan.

John Mark watched Mugface wipe a tear from his only good eye as he took Etan's muzzle into his scarred, calloused hands. He looked into his cat's face, trying to understand what had just happened.

Later that evening, John Mark began reading from the pages that Peter had given him. As he started to read to Mug, out fell Peter's kippah, the little hat he wore when he worshiped. The expression on Mug's face showed what John Mark feared the most—that he would find out that John Mark was Jewish. Mug held his hands up in a gesture as if to ask, "What is all this about, my friend?"

John Mark placed the cap on his head and immediately fell under the power of the Spirit. How long, he didn't know. Awaking from the experience with Peter's kippah, he looked around the room, and there by the bunk was Mugface with the kippah on his head in the Spirit. John Mark just laughed, and said, "Jesus, you were always approaching people, places, and things in your own way. You always do things immediately, at least in my eyes. I shall do my part, Lord, in telling this 'Good News' to everyone."

John Mark knelt down beside Mug, and to his surprise, Mug's face was completely healed. He was still holding the black patch in his hand. Mug opened his eyes and tears ran down his cheeks as he stood up with open arms and hugged John Mark with all his might. They sat together under the influence of the Spirit for a while and basked in its splendor and glory. Yes, Jesus always knows when someone is ready to give all of his or her heart to Him. Mug then replaced his patch over his eye. He would keep this secret for a while longer.

"I am going to leave the ship and go to Cos then on to Miletus where I have family, he told John Mark. He wanted to tell family about Jesus and what had happened in his life. He knew they would become believers when they saw his face. John Mark then placed the kippah and writings back into the pouch and placed them on the small box.

Mugface and John Mark returned to the deck to find perfect weather and strong winds increasing their speed toward their destination. At last, the cry—land ahoy—came from the crow's nest as Fair Haven came into view. As they were coming into port, they heard, "Everyone on deck, now." All scurried, standing at attention, waiting for the orders telling them how to unload the cargo.

Kato followed along. As soon as the gangplank was lowered onto the dock, she was off running in between and around legs of the crew; then she was gone. John Mark looked through his eyeglass and viewed the ships around him. He could see flags on two of the ships, one from Spain and the other from Athens. It appeared that Kato was heading for the Athenian ship, but then she disappeared from sight. "Well, good-bye, little one," he said under his breath.

To the crew's surprise, an unexpected three-day delay occurred because a load of grain had not arrived at the dock. Anxious to see his family, Mugface knew he had to make an excuse to be absent from the ship when she sailed, so he began making preparations. He unfolded his plan to John Mark. "I shall act like I am going wenching. This is my usual habit, so being late and missing the ship will be no surprise to the Captain. God forgive my old ways. I'll not take anything but my faithful Etan. Here is how we will pull this off," Mug said as he gave John Mark a wink.

"When it comes time to load the grain, you will put Etan in a small sack and hide him under your tunic. Then when you go to carry on the grain sack, walk down the pier a couple of yards, like you forgot which way to go and set Etan down on the pier. Etan must not come back on board, so don't untie the sack, but lay it gently behind your feet. Etan won't like this, but he has had many a sack experience in his sea-faring life. He'll just think it's another of my escapades like the many times when I smuggled my grog on board. I always used him as an excuse, in case there were any questions."

Mug picked out a spot where John Mark was to leave Etan. Looking toward the other end of the slightly curving pier, another ship interfered with getting a good view of the dock. John Mark would be hidden long enough to fool everyone.

So, with some extra time, John Mark opened the pouch to talk about the 'Good News' to Mugface. He spoke of Christ's death and ascension to heaven, the baptism of the Holy Spirit, and John Mark's loving, brother of the faith, Peter, who preached the greatest message they had ever heard. He told how Jesus taught by parables. He spoke about the woman who had touched the hem of Jesus's garment and was instantly healed. He related other miraculous accounts to Mugface, including the feeding of five thousand people with five loaves of bread and two small fish, the healing of the man born blind, and the raising of the widow of Nain's son.

Finally, the third day came, triggering a prolific amount of commotion on board ship. The captain could be heard yelling orders from aft to stern while the men scurried about, shouting to each other as they were getting ready to head out to sea. Mugface knew that he must soon make his move.

John Mark prayed the prayer he heard Peter pray many times. "Cast all your anxiety on him because he cares for you (1 Pet. 5:7). God, take care of our new disciple."

John Mark preformed his duties then, according to the plan, left the sack containing Etan at the designated spot. When he returned to the ship, he looked through his eyeglass, scanning the pier, trying to spot his friend. It was then that he noticed Kato. She was moving slowly along the pier. *Where is she going?* he wondered. *She had better get a move on or she will miss her ship again and strand her kittens once more.*

As he watched, he soon realized there were three small kittens following her. "Heaven, help us!" John Mark squeaked and ran down the gangplank, quickly tucking two kittens under his tunic. Making a mad dash for the hatchway, he picked up the other one.

Kato, realizing the urgency of his actions, raced down the stairs and around the bend toward the opening that led to Mugface's cabin. Looking up at John Mark in disbelief, she meowed as if to say, *Don't you believe in miracles?* Letting his heart slow and collecting his senses, John Mark picked up Kato and stroked her till she wiggled and wanted down. "Kato, you've got three of them! Just like the three Hebrew children, huh. What do I do now?" The kittens could have cared less what he thought as they just nursed with vigor and found contentment.

As John Mark awoke the next morning, his thoughts turned to the coming journey. With a good head wind, he would be in Joppa by another morning. While leaving the room, John Mark noticed that Kato had settled down to nurse her kittens once again as if they had never been separated. "God is even good to animals." He smiled to himself.

Entering the room that evening, tired and exhausted from pulling Mug's load as well as his own, John Mark slipped down on the floor next to Kato and started talking to her while stroking her kittens. "Let's see, Kato, if you're going to Jerusalem with me, your kittens will have to have good Jewish names. Hmm, you with the wet looking feet, I shall call you Talia, meaning Dew of God. And what about you, little one, with your mother's white diamond marking. You look like a cute little angel. I shall call you Arella." Now, turning to the little boy and stroking him several times before deciding, "Anissa, my boy, for grace and mercy," and with that, the three musketeers had now become thoroughly Jewish.

Joppa (Jaffa) was the city where Noah's son Japheth had settled, so the people became known as Japhetic. Gentiles. The docking of the ship went very well. The men were anxious to get to their chores completed so that they could head into town for a good, cooked meal, along with fresh fruit, bread, and wine. Captain DeStefano offered John Mark a job any time he wanted and told him that he would miss John Mark's strong arms and commendable efforts at getting the job done. "I learned it from an old pro, right, Peter?" quickly ran through his mind.

The kittens, however, were another story. John Mark had decided that if the sack method worked for Mugface, it would work for him. However, the kittens hissed and snarled at him even drawing out their little claws as he tried to stuff them into the sack. Finally, he was successful at getting all three kittens as well as mother Kato tucked away. It surprised him that the darkness of the sack had a settling effect.

In port, John Mark found a room for the night. On the morrow, he would need to procure a horse for the thirty-three-mile ride home to Jerusalem. He had another problem now though. "How do I travel with my new family?"

The kittens explored their new surroundings, abundant space in their overnight room versus the hole in the wall called a cabin on the ship. They also may have been wondering why they were no longer swaying. *I understand how they feel. I, too, am slowly getting my land legs back,* thought John Mark.

Deciding this was a good time to clean up and shave with hot water instead of sea water, John Mark also longed for a good Jewish meal. Feeling refreshed, he praised God, "Oh, to be on the soil of the land. Thank you, God of Abraham, and thank you, Jesus."

As John Mark entered his small room later that night, he was fully ready for the little cot where he could lay his weary bones. This bed would feel like heaven to him because it would stay put and not sway.

The next morning came early, and as he arose, it was to the smell of breakfast floating through the open window. "Okay, kitties, where are you? Come here, Kato, here kitty, kitty." There was no sound. "No, she wouldn't move them, would she? If so, where?"

John Mark thought immediately of the Athens' ship. Cats have a way of wanting to go home, just like humans. She may have taken them to the ship. "Females do change their minds," thinking about his mother and Rhoda. Starting to leave the room, he noticed a lump of something underneath one of the blankets lying near the leg of the cot. He pulled back the blanket, and there was Anissa sound asleep, warm and cozy. He quickly pulled the blanket all the way off, but the rest were not there. Where? Calling again, "Kato, here kitty, kitty. Blazes, cats, where are you?"

He picked up Anissa and headed for the dock where he spotted a young boy. "Boy, hey, boy, did you see what ship just went outward bound?"

"Yes, sir, it was flying an Athens flag," the lad told him.

Surprised, John Mark thought, *Wow, so it was the ship from the Athens that Kato went to that day. Well, little Anissa, your mother decided for me. She knew that one kitty was enough for me. Three kitties would have been a burden. Thank you, Kato.*

"She left me you sweet Anissa, a reminder of her love, just like Jesus love for all of us when He sent the Holy Spirit at Pentecost. You were named properly Anissa—grace, sweet grace." He then snuggled Anissa close and kissed his beautiful face.

"Let's see if I can find a little cow's milk for you, Anissa, okay? Then I'll need a horse for the journey to Jerusalem. My home place, the place Uncle Barnabas called his second home, became the place where disciples would come along telling stories about Jesus. That began to capture my mind, my heart, and now my soul."

"I can't wait till my mother sees you little Anissa. They all will love you, especially Rhoda and her little ones."

The thirty-three-mile ride to Jerusalem was uneventful. It gave John Mark some time to reflect. He pondered on one impressive event, the time when Peter was jailed by Herod Agrippa. The Church of God had engaged in fervent prayer as a group, praying far into the night. Rhoda was teased for weeks as to why she didn't let Peter in when he came to the door. We all would laugh and hug her, making her blush. "I don't know, Miss Mary. I just ran to get you," she would reply to John Mark's mother.

John Mark continued to reflect on his calling to the Lord's work and the many events leading up to it. His Uncle Barnabas heavily influenced his life. Barnabas was a Levite formerly named Joses; however, the apostles gave him the name Barnabas, meaning Son of Consolation or Son of Encouragement.

Barnabas came with Paul to the Council of Jerusalem when trouble had arisen over how this Good News would work for the Gentiles. After Paul and Barnabas gave an account of their work with the Gentiles, a compromise was reached that satisfied all.

John Mark also remembered Uncle Barnabas enthusiastically speaking with his mother about giving Peter the money he had received from a sale of land in Cyprus. Barnabas was very excited that the money was to be used for the Gospel.

The same was not true for Ananias and Sapphira, and others who had trouble with the giving part, which continues to this day to be a challenge for Christians. The death of Ananias and Sapphira really saddened Peter. He remarked that he fell on his face later and wept. Great fear gripped the Church when the word spread about what had happened (Acts 5:10). Meanwhile many people were being healed and began believing the Gospel message because of the activities of the apostles at Solomon's Colonnade (Acts 5:12).

Often John Mark and his mother would listen to Peter's open, heartfelt remarks. Faith and trust began to build in earnest when the assembly of believers began to form in Antioch, having fled the persecutions in Jerusalem. Believers in Christ first became known as Christians in Antioch, an important city in the Roman Empire. John Mark's spiritual father Peter found himself there building the Christian faith.

The conversion of Saul, who was one of the reasons for problems in Jerusalem, was a welcome message. When God changed Saul's heart, his name was changed to Paul; however, a name change didn't convince all people of a nature change. Many Christians were still afraid of him.

Even John Mark was a little skeptical of Paul because of his conversations with Peter. He still felt, "I can't believe Saul has really been converted." John Mark's Uncle Barnabas helped them all to change their minds concerning this "Paul" who had once persecuted them. Uncle Barnabas kept reassuring them that the conversion of Saul was real. He would say, "Yes, Saul's conversion was real. His name change to Paul is proof. God is in the business of changing lives, so changing our name is an attribute of God."

"We will watch to see the change in Saul's heart, as well," was a comment made among the early groups.

Saul had a lot weighing on his reputation, head hunter of Christians. He made havoc of the church, entering into every house, arresting men and women and throwing them into prison. Saul's actions also affected John Mark's mother and the entire household, sending them into hiding with Philip in Samaria. When Philip went to Samaria and began preaching to the people, John Mark recalled Peter saying that he and John went to Samaria to pray for the new converts that they might receive the Holy Ghost. "Yes, Peter, the power is still in your kippah."

"The city looks beautiful, Anissa, and just up this hill and around the corner should be the lovely, old gate." Pulling the horse to a halt, he carefully slipped his beloved little kitten, Grace, from his pocket to the ground. He then knocked at the gate, waiting as usual for someone to come see who was there. Most of the time Rhoda would answer the door. John Mark planned to hush her excitement and then surprise his sweet, loving mother. Right? Wrong. His mother herself appeared in the doorway, and as she swung open the gate, she exclaimed, "Son!"

"Mom!" John Mark laughed. It turned out to be a double surprise for them both. John Mark's mother gave him the biggest hug ever and then spied the little fur ball on the ground, meowing and looking up at them.

"You were always attracted to strays, John Mark." Picking up the kitten, she proceeded to usher John Mark through the gate and down the small path to enter the big front door. "Son, you look dreadful, but always handsome to me. How long has it been since you had a good night sleep and some clean clothes?"

"Mother, you will always be special to me. Oh, and by the way, Mom, I'll wash behind my ears, too," exclaimed John Mark. The joy of being home and the feelings arising in him were too much to contain, as he did a pirates yell and ran toward the water pot at the back of the room.

Several days had passed, and John Mark knew his mother was waiting for him to start a conversation concerning his life. One Sabbath evening when all was quiet, he took his mom by the hand, and they took a walk down the lane that led to the back of the house. John Mark began to tell his mother a little of what had happened in his life since he left home. "You know, Mother, many experiences have passed through this house.

You can imagine how many experiences have passed through my life. Some have been great, and others were not so good. One that was not good occurred when I left Paul and Barnabas in Pamphylia. At the time they were ministering to the Gentiles while on their first missionary journey. The church at Antioch had given them the right hand of fellowship and had sent them on their way. This event caused Uncle Barnabas's heart and mind to became committed fully to Christ, and he vowed to make the move back to Cyprus when the time was right. He began that missionary journey in his heart before actually moving back to his island.

"If you will remember, at the time I was young, and I guess, afraid to totally yield my life completely, becoming a diehard apostle like Paul. So I left the work and made my way back to Peter. I did, however, want to learn everything I could from Peter. He had been so helpful in my schooling, and my loyalty did belong to him.

"Then fourteen years ago, Uncle Barnabas and Paul went up again to Jerusalem [Jerusalem Council Acts 15] with several others to relate their experiences among the gentiles and to help resolve a dispute concerning the role of the Gentiles in the church. Uncle Barnabas and Paul were to leave for a second missionary journey; however, a disagreement arose when Uncle Barnabas wanted to take me along with him. That's when Paul and Uncle Barnabas went their separate ways, each going in a different direction in the ministry of the Lord.

"In fact, Mother, the joy Uncle Barnabas exhibited when he took me to Cyprus was awe-inspiring. It was then that I couldn't help but notice how much love Uncle Barnabas had in his heart for the souls of that island."

While I was with Peter, he told me of his love for his brother Andrew, the quiet one of the two. Peter talked about how he made fun of Andrew running after John the Baptist; Andrew would smile and say that this was how things work out sometimes, the unexpected happening in an unexpected way. Peter said everyone thought that he was the oldest because Andrew was quiet and would never try to usurp him in any way, demanding his due, saying, "I am the older one here."

"Because of Andrew's quiet and shy ways, people would look past his kind, gentle soul and focus on Peter. Of course Peter always spoke up, which as you know, got him into some trouble with Jesus."

"Peter told me, 'The calling is very important, John Mark. Many are called, but few are chosen.' He told me to listen and learn all I could. In God's timing, His plan for me would be used to further His Kingdom!"

I remember Peter and Anna reading a portion of Psalm 36 to me:

> Your love, O LORD, reaches to the heavens, your faithfulness to the skies. Your righteousness is like the mighty mountains, your justice like the great deep. O LORD, you preserve both man and beast. How priceless is your unfailing love! Both high and low among men find refuge in the shadow of your wings. They feast on the abundance of your house; you give them drink from your river of delights. For with you is the fountain of life; in your light we see light. Continue your love to those who know you, your righteousness to the upright in heart.

"Then they read from Psalm 37 "If the LORD delights in a man's way, he makes his steps firm; though he stumble, he will not fall, for the LORD upholds him with his hand" (Ps. 37:23-24). Peter wept and then finished up, "'The mouth of the righteous man utters wisdom, and his tongue speaks what is just. The law of his God is in his heart; his feet do not slip" (Ps. 37:30-31).

Peter also told me about the time he stayed a few days at Cornelius's home. It was the time when the Gentiles had received the gift of the Holy Spirit. He said he enlightened some of his Jewish friends about how God had given the Gentiles the privilege of turning from sin and receiving eternal life" (Acts 11:18).

"He relayed to me again about that fateful night when he was chained between two soldiers and thought he was dreaming when he saw an angel approach and release him. I remember how excited I was to see him, jumping up and down and giving him a great, big bear hug. Yes, he was my hero then for sure."

"Would you like to hear more of his thoughts, Mother?" "Oh yes, son. Peter was truly a man of God."

Taking out the epistles, John Mark began reading:

> Praise be to the God and Father of our Lord Jesus Christ! In his great mercy he has given us new birth into a living hope through the resurrection of Jesus Christ from the dead, and into an inheritance that can never perish, spoil or fade—kept in heaven for you, who through faith are shielded by God's power until the coming of the salvation that is ready to be revealed in the last time. In this you greatly rejoice, though now for a little while you may have had to suffer grief in all kinds of trials. These have come so that your faith—of greater worth than gold, which perishes even though refined by fire—may be proved genuine and may result in praise, glory and honor when Jesus Christ is revealed. (1 Pet. 1:3-7)

"Mother isn't this wonderful! This is so powerful! I have to say it out loud to wrap my human brain around this priceless inheritance—a gift from God! Citizenship reserved in heaven for all who believe in Him. Eternal life with God."

"Yes, John Mark, from the other pages I'm reading, it looks like he is telling us about false teachers and explaining that their teachings are useless compared to the truth of our Lord and Master. See here what he writes, "So I will always remind you of these things, even though you know them and are firmly established in the truth you now have. I think it is right to refresh your memory as long as I live in the tent of this body, because I know that I will soon put it aside, as our Lord Jesus Christ has made clear to me" (2 Pet. 1:12-14).

"So, Peter really knew his time was ending," she continued. "He was so precious to us. He helped with some of your schooling expenses, and Anna was a great encourager and prayer warrior along with me in interceding for the work of the Lord."

"Look at these statements, Mother. 'But there were also false prophets among the people, just as there will be false teachers among you. They will secretly introduce destructive heresies, even denying the sovereign Lord who bought them—bringing swift destruction on themselves'" (2 Pet. 2:1).

His mother answered, "Peter's life has provided us with a great testimony to the reality on this subject. Remember him telling us about his "errors" while traveling with Jesus? Yes, that must have been a great concern for him. He denied the Lord three times, yet Christ forgave him and transformed him into the solid rock we knew him to be."

"Yes, Mother, and read this. Peter is making very strong points in this second letter he wrote. 'For if God did not spare angels when they sinned, but sent them to hell, putting them into gloomy dungeons to be held for judgment; if he did not spare the ancient world when he brought the flood on its ungodly people, but protected Noah, a preacher of righteousness, and seven others'" (2 Pet. 2:4-5).

"That is powerful, but then he continues,"

First of all, you must understand that in the last days scoffers will come, scoffing and following their own evil desires. They will say, "Where is this 'coming' he promised? Ever since our fathers died, everything goes on as it has since the beginning of creation." But they deliberately forget that long ago by God's word the heavens existed and the earth was formed out of water and by water. By these waters also the world of that time was deluged and destroyed. By the same word the present heavens and earth are reserved for fire, being kept for the day of judgment and destruction of ungodly men (2 Pet. 3:3-7).

"Oh, John Mark, God's Word is keeping this world safe until He comes back again." "Yes, Mother, Peter—as only Peter could—let us have it when he was fired up with the Holy Spirit. Peter would ask us these questions if he were here, 'Have we been too casual? What's the state or attitude of your mind?' I have to continue with this, Mother. These words of Peter's are just so good."

But do not forget this one thing, dear friends:

> With the Lord a day is like a thousand years, and a thousand years are like a day. The Lord is not slow in keeping his promise, as some understand slowness. He is patient with you, not wanting anyone to perish, but everyone to come to repentance. But the day of the Lord will come like a thief. The heavens will disappear with a roar; the elements will be destroyed by fire, and the earth and everything in it will

be laid bare. Since everything will be destroyed in this way, what kind of people ought you to be? You ought to live holy and godly lives. (2 Pet. 3:8-11)

"Mother, why are you weeping?"

"Hearing Peter's words has inspired me to change my attitude to make a sincere effort to whole-heartedly worship the Living God of Abraham with all my strength. John Mark, we need to diligently seek Him with all our heart and live as holy as we know how, for Christ is Holy."

Hearing his mother's words, John Mark hugged her to himself. Her words reminded him of many of Peter's lessons. What manner of person ought ye to be, stung his heart. Seek Him while He can be found. The soul that sinneth shall surely die.

Seeing the tear that glistened on his mother's cheek brought to mind Peter's tear-filled face. John Mark felt himself now weeping.

Gathering his thoughts, John Mark sighed and said, "Mother, I want to copy these epistles for my use and give extra copies to those here in Jerusalem and also one to Timothy. I believe this is the Father's will. These words are mighty powerful to say the least."

"Thank you, John Mark, for sharing your experiences with me and Peter's writings. I shall begin to prepare supper now. You can use the room we built on the roof where your father liked to do his work."

Picking up Anissa and all the loose papers, John Mark ran to the stairs leading to the roof and bounded up them two at a time. It was quiet in this room, and the window overlooked the beloved city.

The weeks went by quickly as John Mark enjoyed the weather, the city, his home and the teachings of "wisdom" he was learning from Peter's writings. As he slowly read through the documents, deep spoke unto deep. The Holy Spirit ministered to John Mark's spirit, implanting messages upon his heart, changing his life. He knew that many lives would be changed by the message God was giving him.

John Mark read the words that Peter had used to end one of his epistles: "Therefore, dear friends, since you already know this, be on your guard so that you may not be carried away by the error of lawless men and fall from your secure position. But grow in the grace and knowledge of our Lord and Savior Jesus Christ. To him be glory both now and forever! Amen" (2 Pet. 3:17-18).

John Mark pondered over these words: warning you ahead of time, losing your own footing, and warning you. Hmm. Questions swiftly flowed into his mind. "How secure am I in Him should the Lord come as a thief in the night? How deeply am I planted in this work of giving out the Good News? What knowledge of our Lord and Savior am I not obeying? Am I doing 'my own will' rather than 'God's will' with an attitude of 'let others do it'? Do I just want to work for money? Do I just want the title of a scribe, nothing more?" The Holy Spirit had put a bull's-eye on his heart.

John Mark went over to the window and looked toward Jerusalem. A heaviness overwhelmed him as he felt all the passion of the important men in his life, the men that built upon the foundation of his life as a young man and had set him on the path he now walked. Jesus and then Uncle Barnabas and Peter. Not to mention Epaphras, Tychicus, and Onesimus. Adding to them, Dr. Luke and Timothy, the mental list went on and on. It included people that were saints and loved ones killed for preaching the Gospel.

Soon people would be reading Peter's letters. Would they accept Jesus? Or would they reject the Good News of salvation as many whom Paul encountered. Some had such hatred for Paul that they resorted to trying to kill him by stoning. Yet, on the other hand, many did accept God's message.

Peter's words were also bold and strong. He had a one-on-one experience with Jesus for over three years and knew salvation was found in no one else because he knew the Lord personally.

No one could claim that the bond between Jesus and Peter was fiction. It was a day by day, face-to-face experience with the God-Man who walked on the earth in the flesh, the very Son of the living God. Any who don't want to believe should consider the truth from Peter who saw Jesus after His Resurrection and beheld His Ascension. He with the other disciples witnessed the power of the Holy Spirit, and all had their feet washed by the very hands of Jesus.

John Mark thought, "I hope those that read Peter's words don't fall away or scoff and say they don't believe. Yes, I, too, saw Jesus and now know that not only is He alive, and my life worth living, but He is Love.

The world accepts living day to day and going about its normal routines, but as Jesus told Nicodemus, 'I tell you the truth, no one can see the kingdom of God unless he is born again' (John 3:3). I, too, gained new life by being born again into the Kingdom of God. As Peter preached at Pentecost, 'Salvation is found in no one else, for there is no other name under heaven given to men by which we must be saved'" (Acts 4:12).

As his mother's friends told the story of the cross and the shed blood of Jesus over and over again, John Mark heard their stories and saw their tears. He recognized the reality of the message. It was not a fictitious tale. One day all will come face-to-face with themselves, their own souls, and the Almighty. Unbelief is hell on earth and blinds people to the truth. It will keep them in bondage of darkness, rather than coming into the light of God's Word and freedom. Although many have chosen to remain in darkness, especially the Scribes and Pharisees, many who have been healed and many of the poor had been accepting the Good News quickly.

John Mark turned from the window after this time of soul searching. He glanced down at Anissa, the foundling cat that was becoming part of his family. He knew that his mother was feeling the attachment as well. His thoughts went back to his time at sea, the ship, Mugface, and, of course, Etan, Mugs faithful cat. He thought, *I wonder if that old sailor made it back to his family?" I'll bet his wife gave him a good whack!* That thought made John Mark grin, as he looked down again at Anissa, who had curled up for a nap.

He scooped the cat up and stroked him gently. "Pretty one, have I been neglecting you? Anissa, do you remember that old pirate Mugface and his rascal cat Etan? Perhaps not—you were just a kitten at the time, but look how you have grown. You know, your name means "grace," and Grace is what these good men I know are preaching—His name is Jesus."

Anissa meowed as if in agreement and then jumped from John Mark's arms. He was hungry and food was downstairs, after all. As he landed, he upset the packet of papers John Mark had there, spilling them about the floor. Many were his father's business papers, listing names of ships, cargos, routes, and so on. There were also receipts for items aboard such as spices, tea, cheeses, and grog.

As he gathered the papers, John Mark noticed a special, larger envelope. It felt somewhat heavy as he picked it up. He could not know at this point that the contents would change his life forever. John Mark paused but did not open the envelope. His thoughts were taking him in another direction, so much so, that he wasn't even aware of walking to the window. As he stood there staring, it wasn't his hometown he was seeing— it was Rome.

He remembered how Paul, who was in prison there, had given instructions to Tychicus, his personal representative who would carry his letters to the Colossian church. Paul wanted Tychicus to take Onesimus, a domestic slave who had run away from his problems, back to the Colossian church. Onesimus now knew freedom in Christ and was ready to return to his home.

Peter was gone now, but Paul understood John Mark's devotion to Peter. Paul had hugged John Mark and was thrilled that the Holy Spirit had helped him to understand the urgency of preaching the Good News. False teachings were beginning to grow in the Colossian church as well. Before they left, Paul laid hands on Onesimus and John Mark and prayed a prayer just for them. He remembered the prayer well. Paul had told the Colossians that John Mark was useful to his ministry and prayed this personalized prayer: "We ask, Father God, that you anoint John Mark with a complete understanding of what Your will is for his life. Make him wise with spiritual wisdom to live a life of worship and honor pleasing to You. Strengthen him to continually do good for others, work to draw all men to You, and never lose the hope of the Gospel. Give him a desire to always be kind. Teach him to know you better each day. You have purchased and paid for our salvation with Your precious blood, forgiving all our sins. We thank you and praise you for this peace found only in You."

Turning from the window with the packet still in hand, he was suddenly aware of his surroundings again, especially the mess on the floor. His father's work life was now reduced to a pile of old records: ships and merchants now out of business, bills of lading, and paid receipts. As a good son, he would be the one to do the so-called house cleaning. His first thought was—why keep them? But he already knew why. He first needed to approach his mother with the idea. Mothers have a way of keeping everything.

On this thought, he returned to the heavy envelope and took out the papers inside. He recognized his father's handwriting right away. His hands trembled, and he didn't know what to look at first. Just then,

Anissa returned from his dinner. John Mark became distracted as the cat began to play among the scattered papers, running over them and sliding underneath them. Anissa was finding the noises they made a great bit of fun.

Returning his focus to the packet, John Mark discovered a smaller pouch inside. Opening it, he found some old maps showing the area where his father had grown up along with a gold ornament, a drawing, and a Jewish dreidel. John Mark picked up the dreidel and gave it a quick spin before turning his attention to the other items. Unsure of which of the papers to begin with, John Mark unconsciously gave the little top a few more spins. Its connection to the Jewish holiday of Hanukkah was a settling influence for him.

As John Mark sat lost in thought, Anissa was intently watching what he thought was a funny bug spinning around on the table. He wondered why this man would be playing with a little bug. But now he had a problem of his own, his head was now stuck inside this funny, brown bag and everything went dark.

Seeing Anissa's dilemma, John Mark said, "Oh, Anissa, let me help you." Once free, the cat promptly settled down to licking his paws and smoothing out his unkempt hair, especially around his ears.

John Mark, in a serious mood now, returned his attention to the map showing Alexandria and Lydia. At the top of the map the name "Captain" appeared. John Mark smiled. Many a time people would call his father just that—Captain. Father, on or off the ships, could pass for the captain, with his straight shoulders, clean white beard, a commanding gait. But that was not his area of expertise, and he knew little about commanding a ship and its crew on the high seas.

"Well, Captain, what will these maps tell me?" Several more times with nervous energy, John Mark twirled his father's dreidel between his fingers. "Where did the years go?" How many times Rhoda and he would sit and play games but now they were adults. The emotion was very heavy even for a grown man's soul to bear, and he quickly returned the top into its envelope, still thinking of his father and how he, as a boy, had likely played with the top and lit the Hanukkah candles.

Next he turned his attention to the gold ornament. With just a few heavy, pure gold links still remaining, it obviously had been attached to a chain. With the hem of his robe, he gave it a quick polish, which revealed ornate pomegranates on the front and a fig tree on the back. "Hmm!" Unknown to John Mark, a secret kept hidden for many years was soon going to be exposed, yet his eyes only saw an ornate pendant, which kept its secret for now. Only a rabbi would know the hidden message that gave safe passage to the owner of the bauble.

Carefully and slowly with trembling fingers, John Mark pulled out an aged document from the pouch that contained the pendant. His gaze fell upon an etching of an elderly, dark complexioned gentleman with long, dark hair and beard, small face, and small shoulders. Age had done its job on the drawing, making the true image somewhat blurred.

"Mother, can you come upstairs please? Whose is this? Mother, did you hear me?" Mary was attending to the entrance rugs, but hearing the tone of John Mark's voice, stopped right in her tracks. "Just a minute, son, I'll be right there," she replied. After straightening the rug, she hurried up the stairs. Drawing a quick breath, she said, "Well, son, here I am. Is everything okay?"

Before she could remark on the condition of the study, her eyes went to her son. He had a questioning look on his face as he held out to her the gold pendant.

Mary gasped. "Oh my, John Mark. You found it. Jacob thought he had lost it! Where did you?" Looking around the room she wondered why she had never found it, and… what in the world happened up here?

"Mother, it was wrapped and concealed in that big brown packet along with a map, an etching, and a dreidel."

"John Mark, this belonged to your grandfather, Rabbi Juda BenTabbai." John Mark exclaimed with surprise, "A priest in our lineage?"

"Yes, son, it's true! He lived in a small settlement in Lydia." Mary continued, "Have I never told you what I know of his life?"

"Not that I recall, Mother," John Mark said with great interest as he brought a chair for Mary. He was more than ready to hear of his ancestors.

Realizing that fact, Mary sat down and began. "I remember the accounts as they were told to me by your father's family. There was an intense dislike for Jews in Lydia at that time, just as we have suffered under the Romans. Your grandfather did his best to follow the Torah but fell in love with a woman from the area who was not of the faith. Her name was Tryphena. The religious precedence was so strong that Tryphena was disowned by her own family."

"The pendant you hold was a gift to Tryphena from her husband, your grandfather, at their wedding. Even though the pendant served as identification for her and proof of her marriage to Judah Ben Tabbai, she kept it hidden most times because of the prejudice. When she found she was with child, they felt it would be safer to move to a little town near Shatby. While living there, they became friends with a local farmer and his wife. Little did they know that farmer would accidently betray their identity to another neighbor."

"One morning, your grandfather slipped away to the barn to study the Torah. From a window, Tryphena saw a man crossing the backyard, heading toward the barn. She thought nothing of it, until she saw the club in his hand. Immediately she felt the fear that those who were under persecution know so well. Instinctively, she quickly gathered a few of her things. She knew she must hide for her own safety and that of her unborn child. There was no way to warn her husband; she could only pray that God would protect them all. Tryphena quickly went to the wine cellar, where she hid herself among the barrels, covering up with boards and cloth bags. She could hear the angry commotion outside and people calling her name. Wisely, she kept still, and as darkness fell, she managed some light sleep."

"Awake at early dawn, she knew it was time to make a move. She slipped out of the wine cellar and moved quickly behind the barn. Huddled there, Tryphena could only pray that her husband had managed to get away as well. She knew she must find a way to escape herself if she was ever to know her husband's fate. She had no plan, and fear was about to consume her when suddenly a snort startled her. She hadn't noticed the young donkey as it quietly approached her. Her immediate thought was, "Thank you, God! Once more *You* have provided for me." Strangely, the colt was calm and cooperative as she sat on his back. He seemed to know exactly where he needed to go as he struck out through the fields."

"You know, John Mark, this account has been handed down through many relatives. Many parts are not too clear. Exactly how she managed to travel all the way to Alexandria and find relatives there can only be God's own protecting hand. Imagine, a young woman traveling alone and with child, no less!

She was taken in by those relatives, and when she died in childbirth, they raised Aristopolus, your father, in the Jewish faith. They started calling him Jacob for they were glad for his birth, which was a miracle. When he was old enough, a relative who was in the shipping business took over his education. Those same relative gave this pendant to him. You know, that dreidle also was included.

John Mark was filled with emotion as his mother recounted the story. "Mother, we have been truly blessed by the kindness and caring of those relatives and priests," he exclaimed.

"How true, son," Mary sighed. "If it were not for them, I would never have met your father while he was here on business, and of course, we would not have had you!"

"Mother, it is wonderful to hear about our family's history. Please continue." John Mark was totally engrossed in this account now.

"Well, the story of your family history up to this point is what I have managed to piece together from what other family members have told me. From here on, I know everything to be true. Not long after our marriage, Jacob decided we would move back to Jerusalem, due to the persecution the Jews were experiencing in the area in which we lived. Many of the people there were from various Berber tribes. Although a few Berbers had converted to other faiths, including Judaism, most remained rather barbarian, and had little use for religion of any sort.

Your father never spoke much about his upbringing, but I knew he missed knowing his real parents. We would take walks on the seashore, and I could tell that he had drifted off in his mind to another time because he had heard nothing I said to him. Of course, he was always very grateful for the folks who had raised him. Oh! And yes, he did tell me about the pendant and how much it meant to him. I was saddened because I had assumed all this time that the pendant and the maps were lost. What a joy it brings that you have found them!"

Mary and John Mark fell silent as the memories washed over them. As mothers do, however, Mary quickly realized that it was late in the day, and there was supper to prepare. Her motherly, "Now who made this mess?" brought John Mark back to the present. As sons usually do, he had a ready response. "Anissa is to blame. He jumped out of my arms, knocking the packet of papers off the table. He's just a kitten and sometimes gets out of control. I'll straighten up here, Mother," he said, giving Mary a big hug.

John Mark enjoyed a wonderful supper that lived up to everything he remembered about his mother's cooking. After helping with the clean-up, he was anxious for some time alone to ponder the things he had heard concerning his ancestors.

"Mother, I'd like to go to the Garden for a bit. Would you feed Anissa?" he asked. "Of course, son. We'll be just fine here." John Mark placed the pendant in his pocket and walked out into the cool evening air. As he walked among the olive trees, their fragrance brought back the memories. Was this the spot where he had felt that raw fear as a teenager?

It seemed so long ago, and yet his memory made it seem as yesterday. The night of Jesus's arrest replayed in his mind as if it was happening at that moment. The tidal wave of his experience washed over him. Nothing could be worse than the death of Jesus and then came the persecution: James killed, Peter arrested and crucified, Paul in a Roman prison, and what of Barnabas? Emotionally exhausted, John Mark dropped to his knees in the Garden and cried out, "Why? What good can come from all of this?"

He began to weep openly as he begged the Holy Spirit to give him understanding and peace.

Through his tears, John Mark now felt able to see the pieces of the puzzle of his life coming together. He knew that his schooling had had a purpose. It would be used to record and further the spread of the "Good News." He realized that time was of the essence; the message must be spread now!

The urgency of that thought caused John Mark to remember a prayer he had heard Jesus pray, "Abba Father, with you all things are possible for those who are called according to your purpose…."

He continued with a prayer of his own, "Lord, I have seen with my own eyes, the faith of many men who have given not only their time, but their lives to serve you. I confess to you that, yes, I will do the same."

John Mark left the Garden quickly, but this time he was not running in fear but rather with a desire to fulfill God's call on his life.

As he approached the gate at his home, he was filled with joy. John Mark understood and accepted God's purpose that was laid out for him. *Ahh*, he thought, *if only Peter were still alive. I'd give that big fisherman a heartfelt hug, and Barnabas too. He always said I would understand clearly one day.*

As John Mark entered the house, his mind filled with questions that he felt his mother could answer. Mary met him almost as soon he crossed the threshold. She was smiling as usual and carrying that spoiled cat.

"My, my, son. You look as if some time in the Garden was just what you needed. Or was it simply my wonderful home-cooked meal?" Mary teased.

"Of course, it was your cooking, Mother," John Mark responded, grinning. "But my stroll did bring to mind some questions I have that are tied to our earlier conversation."

"What are your questions, John Mark? I will answer any I can," Mary said softly. "Mother, I know that Jesus's mother visited here often, and you talked with her at length. I feel I need some details that she may have shared with you. For example, did she mention anything about her other children? Or about Jesus's early life in Nazareth? Did Jesus have problems there when He started His ministry?"

Mary took a deep breath then said, "Slow down, son, that was three questions." With a smile, she continued, "Let's start with the last one. Mary did mention that Jesus had trouble in Nazareth. Folks there seemed to refuse to understand His purpose, or accept it. He was never able to do any great works there, so He moved on quickly."

John Mark remarked, "Peter told me that same account. It's hard to understand."

There was something that still kept bothering John Mark. "Did Jesus's Mother know what would happen to her son?"

"Yes, son, she was told by Simeon when Jesus was just a babe that "a sword will pierce your own soul too." I recall that there was a time that Joseph, Mary and the family went to Jerusalem for the Holy Days. As they left to return to Nazareth, they discovered that Jesus was not with them. He was only a lad of twelve at the time. Imagine their fear and worry! Of course they rushed back to town. They found Him teaching at the synagogue. When his parents questioned his behavior, His response was

'Don't you know? I must be about my Father's business.' His mother never forgot His answer, and I'm sure she knew exactly what He meant. Later on, Mary would want Jesus to rest from His work, but she always knew His answer would be the same as it was on that day. When that came true at the cross, Mary realized the truth of that prophesy. But, on the third day, when the tomb was empty, her joy returned in abundance. The same is true for all of us who believe."

John Mark was anxious now to add this fresh information to the written account he had started. "Mother," he said, "thank you for sharing all this. It helps me to keep my writing as factual as possible."

Mary could sense the urgency in her son's voice, and in a mother's understanding way, she simply said, "You may ask anytime, son."

Now John Mark was excited. "Let me tell you what I'm writing about right now, Mother. The people had been convinced to ask Pilate for the release of a murderer named Barabbas instead of Jesus. The chief priests were behind it all. They knew their case was weak, so they brought every false charge they could think up. Among them were committing treason, using blasphemy, encouraging the people not to pay taxes to Rome, causing riots and, of course, claiming Jesus to be 'King of the Jews.' I've included as many examples of the wisdom Jesus used in answering (and even sometimes not answering) the charges against Him as I know. I've made special notes of His response concerning taxes, using a denarius coin as an example. What a perfect answer!"

"John Mark, I love listening to your thoughts. Could we continue after the kitchen is cleaned up?" Mary asked.

"Forgive me, Mother. I get so caught up in my writing. Of course, I will come and help with the dishes."

With chores completed, Mary and John Mark settled down for more conversation. Mary started things off by saying, "You know, I was thinking about Paul just the other day. Many were afraid of him at one time, but God was able to completely change him. Now, he is a major voice in the spreading of the Good News."

"Oh, absolutely, Mother." The passion in her son's voice could not be missed. "I know of the beatings and attempts on his life. All those, along with his illness, could not stop him from continuing what he knew was his mission. He became a spiritual father to many, I'm sure, but especially to Timothy, just as Peter was to me, after father died. I was honored when Paul asked Timothy to bring me to him while he was in prison. His encouraging words to me about my spreading the message will not be forgotten."

As the weeks rolled by, the time at home with his mother gave John Mark the freedom to continue his writing. Long walks in the Garden and to the market place helped clear his mind and refresh his memory of the events he knew he must record. He also ran into Lesia, who knew Andrew and she was asking if we had any news about him. She was still with Herodias. He told her of his writings. He felt assured that what he had written so far was taking good form, and yet, there was so much more to be done.

One evening, John Mark was relaxing by the evening fire, while Anissa enjoyed a petting on his lap. The aroma of his mother's lamb turning over the fire added to the calm he felt. He began to reflect on his own age. *I'm nearly forty,* he thought. *That is how long Moses and God's people spent in the wilderness.* He was confident that his personal "wilderness" was behind him now. What was next in God's plan for his life? The history he had learned jumped into his consciousness: Joshua—Jericho. Was it time for his own walls to come down? Time to allow God's full access to his life? Time to begin his ministry? Moving to the kitchen table, John Mark unfolded his father's maps. His thoughts rushed through the history he saw there, the town where his grandparents had found the love of their lives. (Was that kind of love in his own future?) Peter and Anna had a wonderful marriage, but then, Paul and Andrew had chosen to walk alone. Uncle Barnabas came quickly to mind, a man totally dedicated to God's service in spreading the Good News.

At that moment, the Holy Spirit began to prompt John Mark concerning questions he needed to answer from his own heart. What did he see the night Jesus was arrested? Betrayal? Yes. Fear? Of course! And yet, only kindness from Jesus. Tragedy? Certainly! But, even so, God's will carried out by a willing servant, as a Lamb to the slaughter.

The questions now became more personal and from deep within his soul. "Am I willing to die for my Savior?" John Mark remembered his own struggles while participating in the mission work. It was difficult then, even with the guidance of those strong and wise men of God. He knew full well that tests and persecutions would come. "Can I do it?" he asked himself. "Am I strong enough?" He knew his mentors' callings—"Peter, feed my sheep"—"Paul, go to the Gentiles." Was this—" John Mark, follow Me," that he heard from his heart?

John Mark remembered when his Uncle Barnabas had received permission from the council to feed the heathen. And then, there was Stephen, a blessed man who served the people with love, and yet he was killed.

John Mark prayed through the night over these thoughts and feelings. By mornings first light, he had his answer. The Holy Spirit had made it clear— he must follow Jesus as Lord, Savior, and Shepherd. He must continue his writings to further the spread of the "Good News." The peace that he felt was nearly overwhelming. He knew his decision and commitment would cause his mother great sadness, but also, knowing her strong faith, she would send him off with a blessing.

The aromas of breakfast wafting up from the kitchen called him downstairs. As he went, he was filled with joy because of his decision, and yet somewhat saddened. He knew it was time to leave his mother's home and get on with his mission. Would Mother understand?

His answer came immediately! "Breakfast is ready, son. I've packed your clothes and a good lunch for you, as well." John Mark was astounded. Mary already knew her son's decision. The smile on her face made it clear. She knew. She approved! This is the way of mothers.

Discussion of the decision seemed unnecessary, so the breakfast conversation turned to lighter topics. "John Mark, what are your plans for Anissa?" his mother asked.

A twinkle showed in John Mark's eye, as he replied, "That old fur ball? I thought I'd just drop him off somewhere."

Mary put on her most shocked look. "Son, don't you dare consider that!" she said.

John Mark was enjoying this now. "Ah, well, you've spoiled him so badly now, he can't even spit at a rat," he responded, tossing Anissa up into the air.

"What do you suggest we do with him, Mother?"

Mary's response started even before John Mark was finished asking. "Why, of course, he will stay with me!"

Now John Mark had everything he needed to start on his journey: confidence in his calling, his mother's approval and blessing, a loving home for Anissa, and a wonderful breakfast. It was time. John Mark gathered his things, and he and Mary walked arm in arm to the familiar old gate. Few words were spoken; neither of them found it necessary. Each knew the others heart, and their tears spoke volumes. "I love you, Mother."

"God speed and God bless, Son."

As he walked down the path, he shouted over his shoulder, "And you, Anissa. You'd best behave or you'll answer to me!" He heard his mother's laughter as the gate clicked shut and whispered a prayer that she would be safe till his return. As she watched her son's departure, Mary whispered a prayer of her own for God to watch over John Mark and bring him safely home again. She picked up Anissa and headed for the kitchen to make some tea.

Anissa (with a mind of his own) decided to head upstairs to look for John Mark. Poor thing, he meowed several times. His meows grew louder, and then he went from room to room, finding nothing but silence. Anissa knew something wasn't right, so he jumped upon the desk to look out the window. He could smell John Mark's scent on a small package and began pushing and patting it till it fell to the floor. You guessed it, the little dreidel came rolling out spinning around and around as if it had a life of its own. Anissa was having his way with it, until it spun off onto the small landing and down the stairs with Anissa in full pursuit.

Mary wondered what was happening with all the thumps and noises she heard. "Oh, Anissa, no, give that little spinner to me. You might swallow it and that would not be good for such a sweet darling. Are you missing John Mark already? So am I! Let's take a walk, she opens the gate to a path around her home, that will be good for both—Now he began chasing real bugs and her flowers got some attention."

Later that evening as Mary was putting the little spinner away, she whispered these words, *"Nes Gadol Haya Po,"* which means "a great miracle occurred here." As she thought of John Mark, tears began to flow. God did do a miracle here today. As she spun the little dreidel, it landed on the side which read *nun.*

"Well," she exclaimed, "I don't have anything to put in the circle!" Her second spin showed *gimel* on the dreidel. A win!—but there was nothing in the pot yet. Gently holding the top in her fingers, she spun again. "Oh my, I must put in half of what I have, half of my bagel will have to do." She chuckled to herself. At this point, Anissa, who had been intently watching the spinning toy, seemed to lose interest. "All right," Mary said, "just one more spin then." The dreidel showed *shin*, which means to pay into the pot, so into the pot went some buttons from the little box on the table. The game had been a welcome distraction for both of them and now it was off to bed.

By this time, John Mark was well on his way to the shipyards. As he went, he remembered his last conversation with the great captain Jack DeStefano. "Come back anytime ye need a job," the captain had said. It would be excellent if they were in port right now. The next day, as John Mark approached the docks, he scanned the mooring spots. Could it be? Yes, there was the flag of Greece and that familiar bowsprit. He could tell that preparation for leaving was underway. He whispered a quick prayer of thanksgiving for God's timing as he hurried over to the captain.

"Sir, I'm back. I hope that you recall your offer of a job if ever I needed it. I would be pleased to sail with you again, if you are willing."

On recognition the captain replied immediately, "ye are a sight to me eyes boy, extending his captain manners along with his great big stature, "willing indeed! Young man, and welcome. Always happy to have a good hand and better yet if ye is sober. So start right now, on that wagon over there. The others have their assignments- ye remember now fasten them tight, so carry on." Yes, he remembers rope burns and how his makeshift bed swayed let alone the cargo down below.

John Mark did not hesitate with his reply. "Aye, sir, and thank you!" The sea breeze lifted his spirits and quickened his steps. He closed his eyes for a moment, both to enjoy the feeling and to whisper, "Yes, Lord, soon I will be outward bound to begin my mission for you, and I am grateful to do so."

That very evening, the captain announced to all hands that the ship would sail to Fair Haven with the morning tide. That meant a good night's rest was in order. The early morning sailing would be a busy time for the crew, what with rigging sails for maneuvering out of port and then again for the open sea. A day of travel and one of loading cargo, along with the sound and motion of waves against the hull of a ship-still fasten- made sleeping aboard a pleasure for now he was not running in fear from the Roman soldiers.

Getting underway the next morning was indeed a busy time, and John Mark had little time for his thoughts. Once the ship had left the harbor, however, he was able to move to the rail for a short break. A brisk breeze filled the sails and also freshened his mind. He stared back at the disappearing coastline with mixed emotions. He experienced deep inner peace, knowing he was about the Lord's work. Even so, he felt a son's loving concern for his mother. *I should have helped Mother arrange those old records in the study,* he thought. But then, he knew she would busy herself with them. A grin crossed John Mark's face as he thought, *Yes, the records, along with that cat I left with her should go a long way to help her with her loneliness.* He knew the truth, though. Her faith would be all the strength she would need.

As John Mark considered his mother's faith, it became obvious. He would need that sort of faith for his mission, faith shown to him by his own mother, Peter, and Paul. "Please, Lord, increase my faith," he whispered.

John Mark's familiarity with the working on the ship left his mind free to think about where his life had taken him and where he was going. His daily duties were, of course, an immediate reminder of his trip from Rome to Joppa and his friendship with Mugface and Etan. He wondered if their paths would ever cross again. There was so much he wanted to share with that old sea-dog if that should happen.

Thinking of the past brought both smiles and sadness. But what of the future? What successes were being accomplished by the others who were spreading the Good News? What was to be his part in that mission, and where was he to start? The questions themselves brought enough anticipation and excitement to make the days of manual labor an afterthought. His thoughts were of the past, though, and old Mugface still seemed to come to the fore in John Mark's mind. More questions—Were they to meet again? Was there more to do and say to Mug and his family? The ship was headed to Fair Haven where Mugface had left the vessel to return to Miletus and his family, so that possibility seemed remote. John Mark turned his thoughts to the future.

At first light the next morning, John Mark was awakened by running and shouting on deck. He quickly dressed and dashed to the main deck.

He heard the Captain barking orders and quickly realized they were changing course to a northerly direction. That meant they would be going toward Cos or Miletus.

Why? John Mark wondered. When he inquired, he was told that during the night, the wind had changed. The captain changed their course to achieve a swifter and easier first leg of their voyage. John Mark was in awe. Could it be possible that he would indeed see Mugface and his family again? Was this confirmation of what he had felt in his spirit? With a silent prayer of thanks, he jumped quickly to help with rigging the sails to catch the winds that would take them north.

Ah, a good captain is like the strong breath of fresh wind blowing into your face as he directs the unfurling of the sails and directs the turning of his wheel. Strong arms and experienced calloused hands always gave everyone on board a feeling of safety. (*Just like Jesus's nail pierced hands,* John Mark thought). Life on a ship is like hard labor with the captain as the task master.

The verbal expletives had to be erased from John Mark's mind; however, he knew that this was the way of the sea. Even Peter initially had difficulty with curbing his language and had to give his tongue to the control of the Holy Spirit.

"Thank you, Lord, for your Son, who is the Good Captain of my soul," John Mark whispered as he lowered a rope to steady an oversized crate. If they had continued to Fair Haven, the chance of seeing Mug again would have been slim. It would have meant leaving the ship and buying or begging passage to Cos, which could have taken days. John Mark began to hum a Jewish tune, *Isn't God Good, Isn't God Good.* He hoped the crew didn't see him hop and skip along the deck. He knew now that God was directing his journey, much as he had with Paul, and that something good was to come from it.

The announcement that their first port-of-call would be Cos was both a confirmation and a blessing to John Mark. The days it took to sail to Cos and dock there seemed to fly by. Unloading the cargo was swift, as well, because the crew knew that speedy work would result in bonuses for all in the form of extras from the cargo of fine wines, wheat, ointments, and silk. During this work, several crew members talked about a tree that had been planted in the middle of the city. It was known as the Tree of Hippocrates and was a sight not to be missed by anyone visiting Cos. John Mark made a mental note to find it if time allowed.

The captain was anxious to set sail for his original destination. As John Mark approached him. Captain Jack DeStefano seemed somehow already aware that this was the end of John Mark's trip. A firm handshake and a quick hug of farewell with words of blessing for a safe journey were all that was needed. It was with much optimism that John Mark turned his attention now to finding his old friend. The local inn and tavern seemed a logical place to start the search, and he could use a good meal and a night's rest in a bed that wasn't swaying.

On his way into town, John Mark came upon the tree he had heard so much about. The reason it was widely talked about was apparent. Right away, no matter where one stood around the tree, another beautiful view of either a landscape or the sea was visible. *Impressive*, he thought, *but what does it mean?*

Before John Mark could give that much thought, he saw the sign for the inn and quickly walked there. As he entered, he was greeted by an old woman. "Welcome, traveler," she said pleasantly. "How may I help you today?"

John Mark matched her smile with his own and replied, "A hot meal, and a bed for the night would be a great start, Ma'am, and perhaps some information."

Yolie pulled a chair away from a nearby table. "Have a seat while I get that meal started. Then we'll see what information you seek." With that, she hurried off to the kitchen. She returned shortly, took a chair for herself at John Mark's table, and proceeded to give him a complete lecture about the town: its history and geography.

All of that was an interesting diversion, but John Mark had to find a moment to interrupt. "You obviously know a great deal about the area," John Mark injected. "Perhaps you know something of an old friend I came here to see. He traveled this way some months ago. You might remember he wore an eye patch and had a cat with him."

"I do indeed remember him," Yolie replied. "Just off a voyage, in desperate need of a bath, both he and that noisy cat. I told him he could stay one night only because of the cat, which he called Etan, if I recall."

"That sounds like my friend all right!" John Mark said. The old, widow woman continued, "It was odd. The next day when he came for breakfast, he wasn't wearing his eye patch, and his eye appeared to be fine. When I questioned him about it, he told a strange story about a 'hat' of some sort and 'healings' brought about by 'angels' of some kind. And about somebody named Jesus."

She was excited now, rushing to tell the story. "At first, I thought it was too much grog talking, but I knew he hadn't had any at that time of day. Since the cat was well-behaved, I allowed him to stay longer. He would sit and talk about his healing experience to any who would listen. He never touched a drop of grog, and I knew that his emotional involvement in the tale was genuine. All of that has caused me to become a believer! But—shhh! The owner of this tavern would not understand, and this is my only livelihood as a widow."

Yolie's excitement with all this was obvious, and John Mark also understood her concern about sharing this Good News and how it might affect her job. "You know, Yolie, this is a great place for weary travelers. Your gracious hospitality and kindness opens many opportunities for you to be a witness for the Lord," John Mark began. "If your motives for sharing are pure, the Holy Spirit will protect you and also bless you through those same travelers."

These comments by John Mark seemed to reassure Yolie, and her smile returned, along with her excitement. "You know, John Mark, other guests have talked about a man who was traveling through many cities north of here preaching this same Good News."

"Ah, yes," John Mark replied, "most likely it is my friend and mentor Paul that they speak about." Taking this opportunity, John Mark shared with Yolie about his travels with Paul and with Peter. His emotion as he did so caused her to comment, "Sir, you miss those days immensely, that is obvious, and I sense that it is time to be about your own journey."

John Mark was amazed by her perceptiveness. He knew it was time to move along with his mission. In his heart, he felt Yolie would become an outstanding worker for God. As he prepared to leave, he found a moment to pray with her for the Holy Spirit's guidance and protection. With that and a huge hug of affection, John Mark was again on his way.

By evening he had made a good connection with a fishing boat heading north to Miletus and looked-for lodging for the night in Palatia. A local man directed him to the only inn in town. As he entered, there was an old man sweeping the floor with a makeshift broom. He seemed unconcerned with John Mark's arrival. "Excuse me, sir," said John Mark. "Is it possible to have a room for the night?"

"Well, stranger, the sign wouldn't say inn if it weren't possible!" snapped the old man. John Mark was taken aback by this response but pressed on. "I'm also in need of some information concerning an old friend I am trying to find."

The man turned to John Mark and his countenance seemed to soften a bit. "Well, sir, once you pay for the room, we'll see about the information you seek," he said. "My name is Ernst, and I am the owner of this place. If there is information to be known in this hamlet, then I am the man who knows it!"

Upon completing the arrangements for his lodging, Ernst offered John Mark a seat. "Now, about this information," he queried.

"I'm looking for an old shipmate of mine," John Mark began. "The only name I knew him by is Mugface."

Ernst could not wait to share his information about Mugface. "Oh yes, I know the rascal you are talking about. He gave me some sermon about repentance and cleaning up my tavern. He went on about how once he was blind, but now he could see. He spoke about a man named Jesus who was crucified and then rose from the grave. All kinds of crazy talk flowed out of his mouth. He talked like a crazy professor, so we stayed clear of him.

Funny thing though, I know for a fact, all about his wenching days and his abuse to his family. I wasn't convinced at first, but he really had changed. The innkeeper paused, took a deep breath, and continued, "One day a ship full of men who had scurvy and even some plagued by a fever came into this dock. Once we learned about what was on board, we all closed our doors and considered the ship quarantined. Not old Mugface. He went on board with his entire family and helped care for the sick. He even got down on his knees and scrubbed the deck. He barked orders so loudly I could hear him from behind my door. He sounded like he knew what he was doing. Once the men recovered, the captain grateful for all his help, gave Mugface and his family a full paid passage to somewhere.

Ernst's face saddened a bit as he continued, "They left on the ship the next day. He didn't say what their destination was." A pensive expression came over Ernst's face. "I wish they were still here," he said softly. "I feel in my heart I would like to know more about this experience he was talking about."

John Mark knew this was the kind of door that Paul would always pray God would open. This door was opened by Mugface. Now all John Mark had to do was water the soil of this man's heart. John Mark prayed, "Lord open his heart to receive your message of the Good News according to your will and in your timing."

While sitting in the corner eating his supper that night, John Mark watched the people come and go in the small dingy tavern. Strangers, yet all people that Jesus died for, not just the Jews, but for all who would come. John Mark now knew what Paul meant when he said he wanted to give his life fully in spreading Gospel and increasing the ministry for generations to come for all those who would believe because we kept the faith and preached the Gospel to all the nations.

John Mark pondered all that had happened in just a few short months. His mind went back to the scenes that were hidden, for they were hard to bear. He couldn't tell his mother that he had witnessed the death of Barnabas. Now he would also face an unknown future; will it include martyrdom? Nevertheless, he knew he would follow in the footsteps of his mentors, for he knew he must be a disciple for Jesus. John Mark had training for the priesthood but following Jesus as a missionary now burned within his soul.

John Mark's thoughts were interrupted when the tavern door slammed open and in barged a loud and crazed man. The man began to yell at him, "You leave us alone!" He began throwing chairs and tables around the room. All the guests were stunned and really didn't know what to do. John Mark remembered Peter preaching about Jesus speaking to demoniacs, and how Peter spoke to demoniacs in Jesus's name and immediately they would flee. John Mark swallowed hard, but as he tried to speak, the words would not come out. They seemed stuck right in his throat. The situation was getting worse as this man was now going to harm the owner of the tavern. John Mark knew what he must do. Just as a chair was raised over Ernst's head, John Mark found his voice and yelled, "Stop! In the name of Jesus

Christ come out you foul demon. Now!" The unclean spirit left the man immediately, and he became so weak he fell to the floor, the chair falling to his side. Silence filled the tavern as Ernst and John Mark looked at each other and at the stranger who was lying as if in a sleep. They didn't have to explain to the people what just happened. Suddenly, the man sat up and began to praise John Mark. John Mark stopped him and said, "You must know that Jesus Christ made the demon leave your body, not

I. Only in His name will the demons obey and only in His name are we delivered." He nodded as John Mark spoke, paused for a few seconds, and then ran to the door, heading for the middle of town.

Everyone in town knew he had been under some spell, and he stopped to tell any who would listen what had just happened to him. All wanted to know how and where this could happen. Back at the inn, Ernst was breathing hard and shaking so badly from all this that he needed to lie down. John Mark covered him up and told him to rest. John Mark himself was in awe to see the hand of God move in such a wondrous way.

He had a feeling that in just a little while the whole town would be at the inn wanting to hear more.

Soon people began to approach the tavern slowly and silently. They came in ready to sit in the rustic chairs or on the floor to listen. John Mark was more than happy to tell them of his personal experience and eyewitness accounts about the man named Jesus. He also shared messages by Peter, James, and especially Paul. Some had heard of Paul as he was much talked about in the streets. The written words that John Mark had put together in a book were now burning fire from his lips as he continued.

John Mark realized this was the fulfilling of the promise Jesus gave to His disciples before He ascended to heaven saying, "Go therefore and make disciples of all nations, teaching them to obey everything that I have commanded you and remember I am with you always, to the end of the age" (Matt. 28:19-20). This commission is why all the disciples were willing to lay down their lives for the Good News. The Lord worked through them and confirmed the message with deliverance. John Mark's first harvest was not in a fine elaborate church, but a dingy, disheveled tavern. Inside were hungry hearts, listening ears, and a chosen one, anointed to spread the Good News.

Paul, Mugface, and others had planted and watered the seed and now God had put John Mark in place to bring in the harvest—a harvest of sin, sick souls: people wanting to give themselves with all of their hearts to Jesus because they knew something great had happened to this town. Others came just to check out what the news was about and responded to the message of truth that John Mark preached. These people were seeking to find a peace in their hearts for forgiveness of their sins.

Other healings occurred on that day as well. Some who were lame could walk again. Several seriously ill ones left for home, healed in Jesus's name. God, who cannot lie, confirmed His Word through John Mark. After several days of sharing and rejoicing, John Mark was able to enjoy the scenes of peace and joy in those who had received and could now rejoice in hearing all of their testimonies.

One night after the crowd had left, John Mark sat alone and pulled out the little pendant. As he held it, his thoughts went to his mother. He recalled her speaking of Alexandria. Timothy had mentioned that Apollos was originally from there. John Mark was also aware that a group of Alexandrians had argued at length with Stephen. *Why was that city so much in his thoughts?* he wondered.

Looking down at the pendant, John Mark realized that the mission of spreading the Good News of Jesus to Jews and Gentiles alike was ordained from the beginning of time. His own lineage, he prayed, was going to be an asset, a key to open doors, as he began to spread the message of God's only begotten Son, the One who came to die to save all.

He knew he must tell them that the God to serve is not their human kings or the idols sitting in their homes but rather a God who is the Creator, both Lord and Savior— the Truth and the light in the darkness of their world. At this point, John Mark knew in his heart that it was time to leave Miletus, and he knew where he was to go next.

The next morning, he shared heartfelt good-byes with Ernst and many of the townsfolk. He felt confident they would continue in their new belief, and that confidence gave him peace.

John Mark went to the docks to book passage for Crete, but this time he would be a passenger. He wanted to share with his good friend Titus his passion for lost souls and what had happened to him in Cos and Miletus. He knew Titus would be helpful in his ongoing ministry. John

Mark said a silent prayer thanking God for all His blessings and asking Jesus to forgive him for not verbally telling Him how much he loved him. "God, please forgive me!" As always John Mark felt in his spirit the peace that only God can give.

The trip to Crete was short, but it gave John Mark the rest his body needed. He remembered that Titus was going to start a church, so maybe that's where he'd go first. As soon as he was ashore, he began asking about the whereabouts of Titus. Several people knew of him and all said that he had started a church in Gortyna. They were correct and John Mark found Titus and his family there.

They were overjoyed to see John Mark and they all talked far into the night concerning what had happened to them. Titus had joined Paul in Dalmatia for the winter and returned with lots of instructions of what was expected of him and the church. Paul exhorted them to not only preach the truth but the entire family should set an example of God's love for the people so they could examine for themselves.

After much sharing, all agreed that some rest was in order. They would certainly remember more to share tomorrow. As John Mark settled down for the night, he suddenly started thinking about his family and how much he missed them. The laughter and closeness became alive in the darkness and he had all the emotions of being alone, yet not really alone, knowing that God was always with him in Spirit.

With those thoughts and the exhausting day, John Mark fell into a welcome sleep, so deep that he did not notice an extra body had joined him on the bed. It sniffed him round about, moved down near his feet, settled in and joined him in sleep.

As John Mark awoke the next morning, he could scarce believe his eyes. There at the foot of his bed lay a cat with diamond markings that were very familiar. *I must be dreaming*, he thought, as he rubbed his eyes. The cat too, awoke just then. "Kato!" John Mark exclaimed, "Can it be? Is it really you?"

Kato came immediately to John Mark for her usual ear rubbing, as if not a day had passed since last they were together. "Ah, old friend, if only we could share our experiences from the past months," John Mark sighed, "what stories we could share."

He arose quickly, straightened the bed as best he could, and hurried downstairs. John Mark was anxious to hear from Titus how it was that this cat, of all the cats in the world, came to live at their home. He was also excited to share the history he had with this particular feline.

This topic brought much lively conversation over breakfast, as Titus's family told how Kato had come to live with them, and John Mark told of their past adventures on the merchant ships. The phrase "What are the chances?" was repeated many times that morning and laughter went round and round the table.

Later that morning, John Mark felt a sense of contentment. He knew Kato had found a good family and that the cat would be an asset to their home as well.

Thinking that it was time now to continue his journey, John Mark sought out Titus for some questions and advice. When asked about a man named Mugface, whose face and eye had been healed, Titus replied that he had heard nothing of it. Titus reassured John Mark that God's plan would always come to pass in these matters. He also gave John Mark an uplifting reminder of what he was to preach concerning family living, doing good always, and trusting God in all things.

John Mark was feeling anxious now to continue his journey. When he shared this with Titus, his friend understood immediately and encouraged him to do so. After some tearful, heartfelt good-byes with the family, John Mark returned to the harbor, where he could book passage on a ship scheduled to leave for Alexandria on the next tide.

From his studies, John Mark was aware of the history of the great city of Alexandria. His own father's business dealings there added to that knowledge. He knew that many gods were worshiped in Alexandria, along with the one God of the Jews. Upon his arrival, he determined to seek out the existing synagogues first thing, hoping that they would be a source of support and a base of operation.

His plan proved successful. The first group he encountered welcomed John Mark warmly. He showed them the pendant early on, and they understood its significance, agreeing to support his mission as much as possible. They too wanted to spread the Gospel message to the idol worshipers of their city.

Once this base of support was established, John Mark began in earnest to spread the Good News, first by speaking to any who would come to listen and also by beginning to instruct others as to how to teach the Gospel message. He knew this was the way to accomplish the mission he had accepted.

He went down to the wharves to get some air, hoping to clear his mind, exercise and enjoy the sea breeze. He enjoyed throwing scraps to the sea gulls and sometimes would relive his sailing days. His routine led to a ministry down at the docks, where ships came in with strangers, some unaware of the Gospel. He used this opportunity to witness to them and preach what he was led to preach. One particular day, a Chinese ship came into port, with a lovely Chinese family aboard. One of the girls was very cross-eyed and had a severe skin disease. She had to be helped by her older sister and her mother, just to get around. Their journey was lengthy but excited to be accepted by the many different countries. This was true again as they came to the city of Alexandria. John Mark greeted them and invited them to the Shul* for a meal. He especially wanted the Lord to heal this young lady. The father was not convinced this could happen or about this new Gospel stuff. He just humbly bowed his head, shaking it side to side and saying—no, no, no. Then John Mark prayed for the daughter with the illness of the eyes and skin condition and God heard his sincere plea. Her eyes cleared and her skin became like new, she was healed! This girl's family and the others started shaking their heads in agreement about the healing as they offered praise to this God that John Mark seemed to know.

Later in the week, as John Mark was busy working on his sermons, his main key point was kindness for all! All of a sudden, the synagogue door banged behind a big, sleazy, flea-bitten cat with a boy in hot pursuit. The boy did not even blink an eye as over the seats and under the seats they both rushed, crisscrossing the room. John Mark was startled from all this noise and when he regained his senses, he went into the big room to see what all the commotion was about. "Whoa, boy," he said. He realized the child could not hear him because he was so focused on what he was doing, which was to get that cat! Suddenly, a lovely young lady opened the door, trying to adjust her eyes from the outside light as she looked around the room. As her eyes adjusted, she spotted the wild child across the room and took off after him. She quickly tried to put her arms around him to constrain him and instead got smacked in the face by swinging arms.

Move, man," thought John Mark, *move! Why are you just standing and watching this episode? Move man, move!* He grabbed the boy with a swift quick jerk. The child knew he was to stop, and stop right now. The young lady was now rubbing the red mark on her face, making sure that her eye was okay. The tears told the rest of the story. "Sorry, bishop," she said, "he has been this way since childhood. John Mark froze for a minute as he beheld her beauty. She had soft-looking olive skin. Black hair framed a well-proportioned face, with a perky nose and rosy lips.

Suddenly, John Mark was startled as the boy started kicking him in the leg, and by all that was holy, the sermon on being kind was all but forgotten—there was going to be one less child on this God given earth! He got behind the child and wrapped his arms around him and just sat him down right on his lap like a baby. Meanwhile, the beautiful sister had cornered the cat and wrapped it in her shawl. We both just looked at each other and began laughing. "We make a good team," she said.

Oh my soul, an angel with flowing black lovely hair and a devil, all in one day—went through his thoughts.

The boy child (now quiet) looked finally at his sister who came and sat down beside them both. Would you believe that cat actually was gentle now? This reminded John Mark of cat Kato and how the lesson of being kind was not just for humans, but for all animals too. He thought of his mother and how she would always scold him for bringing strays of all kinds home.

As the young lad stayed calm, he was happy to touch and pet the cat that laid in her lap. She was also looking at me at the same time which made me feel a little embarrassed. Me? Head bishop of this town, sitting on the floor with a little brat, a flea-bitten cat, and a lovely woman. God does have a sense of humor! What would the second bishop think if he were to come into town to visit the most holy of all the places?

She must have felt it too, because all of a sudden, she started to apologize. "Oh, I am so sorry. My name is Rose Mizeall and this is my little brother, Landon. We came into town to see an aunt off to Athens." As Rose was explaining what she was doing there, all of a sudden Landon took off again after that cat.

"Why is Landon so obsessed with that cat?" asked John Mark. Rose explained that they had a farm, outside of town, and Landon probably wanted to take it home with him. He sleeps with several of his different animals on the farm and they seem to sense that he has trouble hearing and understanding; he gives them a special kind of love from within himself. Once he was awaken by one of them licking his face and we found a poisonous snake in the room. The bigger cats made quick work of catching it and you can imagine Landon pointing and screeching trying to explain what he must have been feeling.

The hour was getting late, so before Rose collected her things, John Mark wanted to share his love with her about Jesus and the healing that took place earlier. "No, bishop, we don't believe in anything like that, I'm sorry," Rose said. She showed a quick change of facial expression as she took Landon's hand and motioned with her eyes for him to come and right now. As Rose waited, John Mark asked, "Where outside of town do you live?" John Mark hoped that she didn't go out of his life as quickly as she came into it. Maybe she doesn't believe in love at first sight?

Getting up off the floor, John Mark began to wonder about his day earlier and wondered, *Why the Lord did not allowed him to heal the child?* Slowly he ambled to his desk and decided to include this little lesson into his talk tomorrow.

The next day came early and in his morning teaching he said to his people, "What can you do to help the deaf and dumb children in our area?" The outcome was pretty simple—Practice what you preach went through his heart. So on Tuesday, John Mark told Bishop Ronnie he was going outside the town to look for the poor and children who needed God's help and just maybe he would find Landon among them. If the peasants didn't want to come to town then he would take the Lord to them. Yet God knew that the timing for him to do this full-time was not yet to be.

His sleep was being disturbed knowing that Jesus had given to the disciples the ability to heal in Jesus's name. Rose just didn't not know what she had walked out on—let alone his admiration rising up inside of him. Was she already promised to someone or engaged? Was she destined to be an old maid or maybe she was married? Questions unanswered that would drive him crazy. He hadn't thought this way about anyone since Petronilla was abducted from the brown door, the catacombs. Hearing from Titus that Anna, and Petronilla were killed sealed his heart. He focused on the lost souls and his calling to preach the Good News.

He walked through the small populated area heading toward the blacksmith's area to get a horse to ride instead of walking. Mr. Bo'ney an older horse please, so I can ride out of town instead of walking. Sure son, anytime and here is old Lucy girl. She also knows the way to come home if you forget. Laughing his warm laugh and jesting toward his small but neat little barn. He was the blacksmith for the town and very well loved by everyone. He came on and off to services. He saddled Lucy and John Mark was on his way. What a beautiful day and somewhere in his heart a song was making connection.

One of his parishioners seeing him on Lucy laughed and yelled finally someone getting you from the duties of the faith. He wondered what would happen if he kicked Lucy slightly in the ribs, no better not try it, laughing inward—she just might let me know she has some fire left. He went quite a ways and was disappointed he did not get his self up from the floor and stop her to know just how far they lived—but he didn't so this is what it is. He wiped his brow then realized he didn't bring anything to drink. What has happen to his skills? He was about to turn around when who came riding up the road on the magnificent Arabian horse—one that was black and full of fire. One like his eyes have never seen. Rose, and he on Lucy oh no.

If the ground would open up, he would dive in. "Well, well, bishop, what brings you so far out today?" He knew then what his great manly physique on an old horse looked to her. Tongue tied for a moment, he said, "My dear, I am looking for you on my humble beast since you did not let me know where you live. That will get her, being humble for right now she is the power of gloat and impossibility."

"My dear bishop, I am sorry but maybe your God ought to provide you with a chariot and 6 horses."

What? How could I have thought beauty also came with a heart? I am not a Roman.

Hey, woman!"

"Well, she doesn't know I have sailed the seven seas—fought off—it didn't matter she flung her hair back—turned her black steed around and left a trail of dust in my face. Woman!!! I can sign divorce papers in my priesthood—I know what I can say, I see myself giving out—one!!! Shouting through the dust. "Come on, Lucy," she didn't hear me, "let's head home."

Dropping the reins around the saddle, he let Lucy have her head, and sure enough, they arrived back at the barn.

"Well, that was not too long of a trip may I ask what happen?"

"Sorry, Mr. Bo'ney, I realized I needed some water and the preaching in the pulpit life has made me a little soft—if you know what I mean. Tomorrow maybe I will be more prepared and will stay out longer. Do you know who might own a beautiful Arabian thought I saw one at a distance?"

Oh, the clan that came in from the northern part, Afro-asiatic families— stolen too. Folk say Roses' mother was taken and made a slave, but the boy is part Berber—Mr.

Bo'ney kept talking. While John Mark's mind was in meltdown.

Rose and Landon, different, feel sorry for the boy and her. Those men are quite harsh chicotter," utter Bo'ney, part French himself. (Francophone)

You mean, whip, beat children? He has noticed their fear, but this kind of nomadic people made his father and mother leave Egypt. A wound reopens now-concerning his family. The thieves that killed his father also were not caught, and Rose, her heart was going the way of that clan. His heart right at this moment was not in a Jesus mode.

Later at night, Rose was laughing to herself about the pious righteous man on an old horse, yet inside her, she felt kind of a conviction. After all they did hear he was a Holy Man. She was surprised that he was younger. He had been mentioned several times around the camp fires during the harvest time. We are strong people her uncle would say and we will not give up the land we have taken is that clear, and the grog would flow with ayes. Our God is what we can do for ourselves. Her horse was stolen and she did not even inquire about the owner. Why were opposing thought waves coming now—maybe it has something to do with the bishop—he might have cast a holy spell on me? Or he is a good witch doctor. I will shake it off, taking her tambourine she began to dance—signaling the other women to join for the night was airy and sweet.

The following days she rode out to the spot where he had been. No show. Good and good riddance to the devil himself. She began to race her horse faster and an attitude was developing of a dare me to dare. Her uncle began to mention something to the clan. So they took Night Storm from her, thinking she is going the way of the moon. Landon would stare at her wondering why suddenly she was so moody and not her happy go self.

A plan was born calling Landon to her side she hands sign tomorrow you and me go into town see if some big ships are in? We could look for the cat again. She then remembered the one dress she wanted to wear was soiled. She went and got it. Plot, plot, into the water bucket working arms up and down for a few minutes—a good wringing then laid it outside to dry. Early morning smiling now she went to check on Landon. He noticed that she had a twinkle in her eyes. She was again soft spoken and making sure his hands and ears were clean. *No*, thought Landon, *she is going to the temple.*

John Mark was having trouble every day himself. He was a pouting down in the mouth character. "Are you feeling ill?" Bishop was asked several times from several different people.

"Yes, I am ill. I want to get back at a witch went through his brain."

"Bishop, we have a young lady here with an ox for you. She brought it all the way from her farm. She said it was for you to sacrifice which you Jews do." Why did a part of him have steam coming out of his ears and another part of him wanted to roll with laughter. Game playing—well, two can do that dance. He put on his white robe and placed his necklace around his neck and his kippah on his head. He stepped outside the church doors and with the most Holy of Acts was thanking her beyond measure for such a generous gift.

"You must stay, and after we slay it, we shall have a good feast." It was not making him angry so she quickly turned her wagon around and off she went again with his royal bishop holding the reins to an old one horn ox. Points zero to two blast her he mumbled. The crowd that was gathering was murmuring, "Is he really going to kill the animal?" He had been preaching that they do not do that now because of the Good News. He assured the people with she doesn't understand the Good News Gospel.

And what he was preaching was the way of grace not the old law, so we will accept this nice gesture as a nice gesture. Under his breath, "Yes, a nice gesture to try to get me to kill her. Lord, Mary Magdalene had only seven devils in her—this one has a Berber."

Now with quiet time before bed, he decided he should pray and rebound because of his mental attitude sins. "Why does a part of me want to grab her and hold her like the way I did the child? The child, Lord, I am so sorry. He is important to you and I am looking at my own flesh and my own anger. Please, Lord, work out this situation with them before I do something foolish like locking her into a cage and placing her on the one horn ox in the public square."

Days went by and things appeared to return to the norm, yet he found that a burden for the poor children growing stronger in his heart. He now went out among the townsmen taking food, clothing, shoes, and wine. He found that healings were being manifested and he was wondering at the new things God was doing in his life. He really loved it when a crippled leg was touched and a wrinkled hand was unfrozen and set free. He rejoiced as his sermons even began to show power and strength. From the people, he was seeing miracles being done. Yet, alone at night, his thoughts would drift toward her and Landon. She too drove herself into the summer and late fall harvest. She even try weaving and baking. She realized that she had made herself a kind of toga and under garment. Yes, one that covered her arms and legs and was fit for the temple. She yet could not seem to get the wagon and go into town. She froze inside—a holy man—what would he want with her. She could be a lady of the night but never yet cross that boundary and once when one man tried her uncle slit his throat. She never was going to ever settle with any man as they were all nothing to her eyes. She had planned to escape on one of the ships and sail away, but Landon always brought her back to her destiny and reality. Who would see after him, not his uncle. Twice he had whipped Landon for not hearing. He then shoved him at her and said you take care of him or we will. Now it is her daily chore. Landon yearns to ride like the other kids and go hunting. No, Landon has a hard life ahead of him. Maybe when he is another year older, they both would escape to another place. She has been looking for that escape and she lied to Bishop about having an aunt and leaving for Athens.

The weather was getting a little cooler and the dress was going to be perfect for her. She would have to wait till her uncle and the other men went off to do their thieving. She would take Landon and some vegetables to sell as a decoy. She also was getting nervous in thinking about sitting in on a service watching him. Now to put the finishing touches on the undergarments she added some stolen ribbon.

Landon got a new belt and shirt. She was a little surprise how sewing was coming so easy for her. Then her Uncle remarked looks like you have the gift of your half breed Jewish mother. Mother it seems like eons since she thought about her and how far away her grave is now. She as a young girl, lived with her mother when her mother was forced to take off with the new person who passed through the small village so far south in Libya. Landon was her half brother and that is another reason that to have him show weakness was like a blow to the ego of the Berbers. Mother illness was probably from being abused after an illness as women were to be powerful like their men. This was the driving force to her tough character. She could win the fighting contest, the knife throwing, the horse riding, the kicking and one more a killing test which will soon come. Now she can do the sewing, cooking, yes. She showed them that she may not be the child of a Berber—she was better.

Excitement to say the least was the feel of the day. Landon was excited to be going somewhere, and he motioned to his unusual sign, the cat. Yes, we will look for him. She decided to drive the old wagon with the good ox. Mr. Holy doesn't know that she got into trouble for doing what she did and ended up with a fight to show face. She took several good blows but so did her uncle. He laughing spit out loudly, "Look everyone at the meanest woman on earth. Drink up. Someday she will be running the whole show."

She knew he lowered his stick and she was smart enough to take advantage of it. So she also knew to push him would be of no good for her.

The sun was shining even though the air was cooler. Refreshing now. She had begun to dress very much like the men around her since she didn't want anyone else getting his throat cut. Once in a while, she gets sick thinking about all the blood. Now the new dress was so darn uncomfortable but a lady she'll be.

She saw there was a space behind the synagogue building and drove around in back. She fastens the stake to the ground and the ox could get a little grass by the wagon. She again fussed with her sleeves, her neck collar and the undergarment. Landon started laughing. It makes you look funny. She ignored him and motioned him to move beside her. They entered together into the door way and quickly she took a seat in the back by a little window. Landon bent down and looked under the seat and then climbed up and sat down. Higher than what they were use—maybe they should move toward the lower benches all arrange in order. Landon was glad for now his feet could almost touch the floor.

Finally Bishop Mark appears so splendor was his Sunday dress. She left out a gasp. She realized others were seating themselves with their individual families and she knew she had done exactly the right thing with Landon. She also was taking notice of the dresses of some of the women and of the men and children. She could tell that some were better off and some were very poor. She was assured that they didn't have an Uncle bringing home certain borrowed articles. She then turned her eyes toward the front. Bishop had finally realized that she and Landon were there. He froze for a moment. The sermon came from his lips and was so elegant that she was sure he was not human. The simple story of a man called Jesus. That was the person he had asked her if she knew. No, she could not remember meeting a gentle man like the one he talked about.

People then began to come forward and he let them break off small pieces of bread and a sip of wine. She wondered what kind of ritual that was and why?

She could understand eating but in church, *hmmm* maybe that is why everyone comes. But such small portions no, she enjoyed larger portions at home.

She then realized how her education was badly neglected, another reason to leave this wicked clan, sooner rather than later. The world was out there, and she was going to go and Landon with her. Bishop then began to sing and pray and now, he motioned for me to come forward. I shook my head no, but he then pointed to his ears. Oh, he wanted us. I shook my head again,—don't think we want any part of that bread thing but thought that part was over? Then I felt like someone else was lifting me out of my seat, and it was so peaceful as both of us walked toward him, yes a healing call was in place for her and Landon.

Bishop then smiled at me and my heart thumped and I had to swallow twice. He then took Landon's face into his hands for he knew Landon was about ready to dash out toward the door. He knelt down to be eye to eye with the child. He then did something else and finally he spoke very loud and commanded Landon to hear and to speak. I jump back out of fear but Landon began smiling and smiling and then open his mouth and started singing. His voice was like an angel, and everyone started clapping and dancing and laughing and rejoicing. I stood I am sure with my mouth open if I had not witness it I would not have believe. I had heard that he was the Holy Man, and now I was ashamed for some reason for calling him a witch doctor. I could not stand there so I turned to run and he caught me by the arm. Wait, Rose, wait, God wants to do something for you. Let all the hurt go for he cares for you, and when he took me into his arms, my tears started flowing. Crying was the number one *no* in our clan. Yet I could not hold them back, and with his arms holding me, the best part of love is finding it.

We began meeting and he began to open the Good News to me. His life and where he had come from Jerusalem. Its beauty and its horror with the Romans. He then told me about his mother and how his Great Grandfather had found love here and that is why he came. I smiled and was so glad the clan was chased out of the last town—they will bully and plunder forever if they don't meet this Jesus.

John Mark said more need to hear the message of change. I then express the desire to get away meanwhile Landon keeps the secret of his hearing well, but he started to sing the other day I am very afraid of the end results. No one heard him this time, but it is only for now.

He agreed with me that leaving would be for my and Landon best interest. He has taken a vow to minister here in Alexandria and God had moved him around the Africa Areas. If God chose change again, he could be back in Jerusalem doing more writings.

Schooling was upper most in his mind for me, as schooling was greater in his life than other things.

He expressed that for my signing gift to help others on a bigger and better scale, it was necessary.

God expressed a desire to have people be happy because of His love. He then showed the pure gold locket now on a new chain. The secret red threads the scarlet line that told so much to those who knew the story of Joshua and Jericho. It saved Rahab and her family. His mother will recognize it, and she and her brother will be safe. Landon is young enough and with his healing he will catch up quickly. He then held me tight and stroked my hair away from my face as well as the tears. Again, I try to say that just living here would be, but down deep the desire to get away from this place was there.

No, Rose my vow along with the others—toward Jesus—is meaningful to me. Vows get broken too much and are just then meaningless words. No one should make one without truth to you, remember I see in you a lovely treasure worth appreciating. You are very special to me. Holding was all the words needed to make me want to accomplish the best that God had for me, I vowed to myself not to let this wonderful handsome and kindness of all men, down.

Plans were made with Mr. Bo'ney. You will bring your horse in for shoeing. I know a certain captain and only he will I allow to take you to Athens and then to Joppa. Landon will have to be instructed to play along as this depends on both safety of you and him. Now let me teach you a prayer that Jesus had us pray. Now let us pray, Our Father in Heaven and Rose signed.

It seemed like it was only yesterday that she left. It was the hardest thing for me to physically do but to live for Christ is gain and I just couldn't break the heart of God nor Rose's.

7

Letter

My dearest son,

Just a short letter—letting you know I am very proud of you and the news of God moving on the heart of the people. I was not surprised that the ones you sent home *were homeless and needy and loved cats.* Anissa and Landon are inseparable.

We have, with Rose gift started to help a few deaf children.

Her hand signs seem funny. Landon really has the cat one down good, the children love seeing his hands do that one. We are making our own small charts.

Thank God for touching Landon, he is very bright and has a lovely voice. Rose is a great help to me. Both are doing great with their school work. Rhoda's oldest son Benjamin, is very smitten with Rose, but Rose doesn't even see this. She said you *preach like an angel.*

The pendant again is back in a safe place. Oh, by the way, I Finally got rid of papers, makes a great room for Landon.

Stay safe Shalom.

Mother

Time began to go swiftly as more and more services were completed. One night after communion, his heart had the yearning to head down to the docks. A ritual now that he loved for the sea breezes gave him peace and pleasure. To hear the waves pounding off the wharves. He could look across and see old ships in for repair and new ships embarking in and out with their cargo. His availability to help with strangers.

What was disturbing him now? What did he want to discover or learn from this earnest strong desire to look? To look for what? To look for whom? Maybe that was it. Looking for whom? Rose and Landon, I know are safe from the letter. Mugface was visible in his memory. Mugface and Etan. He had the puzzle piece Kato and Anissa but not Mugface. Why did my life let me run into him and why did my heart love that old man. His whole soul filled with an uncanny abundance of amazing love. Is Mugface coming here? He started walking swiftly down the pier, turning his head so that his eyes scanned the tall ships, the small boats. Lord, what is the meaning of this emotional upheaval on my being? Mugface, Etan, he called out into the rustic air and only sea gulls answered back. What is the meaning of this realistic desire to look for a face?

It was at this moment that God through the Holy Spirit manifested himself to John Mark saying, "This is what I am doing. I am looking for the Mugfaces of the world to come into my kingdom. I am scanning every name who accepts my blood—bought ticket to heaven. My shores have more room and today while they can, I want more to come. I want more to believe, and I want no one to be lost. You must now go out among the peasant people and be strong. Be firm in telling them, 'Today hear, today see. Today is their salvation.'" John Mark froze with that revelation, Revelation of God's Love. He knew what he felt when Mugface was not found—now his senses were back to normal. He knew then that God would feel strongly more than he did in the Revelation Lesson. Revelation Knowledge that John Mark experience *hit* him which there is no words to describe it—sad lost feeling filled his soul making him sick to his stomach. Revelation Knowledge is realized for the *truth* in lives not being found. Lives not among saved ones will be indescribable. Every soul not found grieves the *heart of Father God. The Holy Spirit will grieve.* His mind flashed back as a young lad, how Jesus would look at him with such Love in His eyes. Those very eyes will be looking for special faces. He then saw Jesus on the cross; a price was paid for *this free ticket.*

He slowly headed back when he noticed the flea bitten cat sitting on a small boat. "So, my friend, this is where you live. Sorry your life did not change," Rose said. They called you but you would not come." Memories of a cat and rats and his saved legs jarred his mind. Suddenly the old cat darted down to hide. Hiding from danger is one thing but to hide from the faithful caller the *Holy Spirit* calling for a *chance* for change, lost, lost, lost. His usual habit was to polish the gold locket chain, but now Rose has it.

The scarlet thread woven secretly in the fig tree now is her and Landon's safety. He knelt for prayer and ended with saying not my will but yours Father. He then re-hung his bishop habit in the closet. Walking slowly through the building in the dim lighting and silence toward his bedroom, renewed his vow to keep preaching firmly one God, one Jesus, one Holy Spirit. John Mark set out the following days, preaching loudly and firmly: ONE GOD, ONE JESUS, ONE HOLY SPIRIT. He finally encounters the idolatrous pagans on an Easter Holiday. They dragged him from his synagogue in Bokalia (the place of cow), east of Alexandria on the sea shore. When death came to change his path, his salvation ticket brought him to the arms of Jesus.

John Mark was given sometimes by the religious writing a bad rap or an off viewpoint of being no good for God's kingdom. This came from a dispute with Apostle Paul and his uncle. I found him to move from a frighten teen to a strong and wonderful servant of God. I enjoyed writing about him and how he matured toward his calling to God, his love for his mother and his uncle and finally for Apostle Paul and Timothy. Research shows Egypt loves you and so do I.

God will be looking for faces, yours, mine, our households and neighbors. God will be looking for whosoever may come. I renewed my ways for I *want* the arms of God for the final trip.

What arms do you want? I am now asking you to *change* as I did. *I had a choice of two ways!*

Purchase a faith ticket or dart away and not answer the call.

Prayer: Please, God, forgive me of all my sins and write my name on the passenger list that God will have in heaven called the Book of Life. Let me turn my life around and be loving to family, friends, care for the earth and the animals thy will be done. Amen.

Please sign this book knowing your signature shows that God *will see your face. Then share it with someone.*

Shalom
Pearl M. Smithern

PART III: ANDREW

Jacob Barjona

Jacob Barjona looked at the threatening sky and knew he had to hurry with his loading. He threw on the last barrel of salted fish, spilling brine over the floor of the boat in his hurry as he shoved off from the shore of the Sea of Galilee. Time after time, he and the sea did the dance of the last load. Fish that were carefully kept in water for freshness brought in a better price. He knew many customers would be waiting to buy them for their supper just before the solemnity of the Sabbath.

His thoughts were pleasant ones on this quickly fading day with the prospect of what this load would bring. His daughter's wedding had set him back a little. His sons, Simon and Andrew, were growing like weeds, but soon he would have his sons to help in the business—Simon with his strong arms for pulling in the nets and Andrew with his quiet smarts. He had sent Simon to Bethlehem to work for a distant kin tending sheep. Simon loved the sea as much as he did when he was a lad and hated tending sheep. Soon they would all work together. Yes, he was enjoying the future in his mind.

Jacob's wife was feeling poorly when he left for work that morning. He assured her that he would bring Simon home quickly. He lingered before leaving this time, kissing her tenderly, and said, "Soon, Simon will be back to help with fetching the water and with the other chores. Rest, my love, today. I will be back as soon as I can."

With the fish counted and delivered, he arrived home later than he had planned. The day's fish soil was definitely embedded in his clothes and under his nails. He undressed quietly, and with what water was left in the water bucket, he doused his head and body. *This will hold me till morning,* he thought. He moved quietly, not wanting to awaken his lovely wife. She always fussed over him, but she didn't need to when she was ill herself. He lay down in the living room as exhaustion overtook him. His slumber could be heard throughout the whole room.

The dawn brought a cruel awakening. The room was very still and cold. The fire had gone out; only silence greeted him. His awakening senses brought alarm as he looked about the room. Stillness prevailed; the unthinkable had happened. His precious wife lay still and motionless. She was gone!

Simon and Andrew wept beside their father as they placed their beloved mother with her ancestors. Jacob was deep in thought. "Father, are you feeling well?" asked Simon. Jacob didn't answer. Who would help him raise his two motherless boys? He would need help. Jacob's distant kinsman, Salome, wife of James Bar Zebedee, came to mind. She had two boys of her own. Could she care for two more? His heart was heavy as he contemplated what the future would hold. He decided now was the best time to take the boys to Salome. She had said she would keep them for a few days, giving him some time to figure out what he wanted to do now with his fishing business and his wife's articles of clothing.

With the boys out of the house, Jacob stood in his living room in silence. He picked up a sturdy, old box from the kitchen and slowly proceeded toward the back bedroom. It was hard to just choose one item over another, giving up precious items of his dear wife, but what would a man do with woman's apparel? While looking at Huldah's possessions, memories of times past flashed through his mind. But now he would just have to accept the fact that he only has memories and his only option will be to store these memories in his heart forever.

Looking at the bits and pieces of a lifetime, Jacob found that his faithful wife had saved the boy's homemade things, and for herself, she had pressed an old flower between the Torah's scroll. Wiping a tear or two from his eyes with the sleeve of his shirt, his mind kept on racing for the why. He could not understand the reason. His wife was always so strong and never grumbled. So why had she died? He wanted his life back to normal. In Huldah's words: leisure enjoyment and lovely sunsets. Oh, yes, and lots of grandbabies. This latter thought made him smile.

He suddenly remembered the one important thing he had left undone, which had to get done now—the taxes. He had to stop over across the way to Capernaum, to report in and pay them. He remembered an old friend and his wife that lived over that way. He knew from his acquaintance with them that they would surely accept and appreciate Huldah's things. He would pay his taxes and then take the box to them. Romans taxes on top of the hard work ate away at the small income of every fisherman.

Pressure from former debt and the current need of giving money to Salome for the upkeep of the boys kept growing inside him. He decided that an all-night and all-day fishing run was the thing to do. Yes, he would do a fishing marathon. He must.

Just before closing the box lid, he placed into it Huldah's favorite sandals. She was always careful not to wear them out in adverse weather conditions. Another hidden memory for now. Looking around the house to make sure the lattice windows were closed and that he had not forgotten the bag of money for the taxes, he retraced his steps back into the bedroom to get the box. Placing it under his arm and sideways on his hip, he headed down to his boat.

The heaviness of mourning a loved one and now needing income were two devilish driving forces, a mixed bag of emotions in a strong fisherman's soul. He felt the sunshine on his face as he walked down the worn old path. The blue sky and calm shoreline were inundated with the noisy activity of the gulls overhead. This made him start feeling better inside as he drank in the sea air. Ahhh. So refreshing to a fisherman. Yes, a super catch would be a great solution to his problem. The dance of the last load was far, very far, from his thoughts on such a lovely day. His strong arms maneuvered the boat out away from his special, little, rustic, homemade dock.

Later during the middle of the night, a long way from Capernaum, a long way from the elderly couple, a long way away from his boys, the weather turned into an unexpected, violent storm. Frequently, storms would come up very quickly on the Sea of Galilee. Did he ignore the signs? Did he think he could get in the last dance? The pressure of life clouded clear thinking into poor judgment—to stay and to stay fishing, taking a chance. The small fishing boat that had been tossed to and fro washed ashore the next morning without the sweet fisherman with a good heart, empty of its captain. Jacob was now with his lovely wife.

2

Meeting Leisa

Salome, the wife of Zebedee, not only took in Simon and Andrew but loved them like they were her very own. Her two hot-headed and stubborn sons also adopted the new additions to their family as blood brothers and enjoyed arm wrestling and other mischievous play.

However, Salome knew that it was not always going to be all fun and games. The boys needed to be taught many things concerning the fishing business and getting this information into them would be the challenge. Most of all though, they had to be taught to follow the Sabbath rituals. Even with the additional work of two extra mouths to feed, this chore along with many others would still fall to her.

Barjona's boys arrived at a busy time in the midst of the fishing season, the highly pressurized time of salting the fish, preparing for an order going out on a ship to Rome. Much effort was needed to balance the delicate timing, to keep the fish fresh and to get them to the shipyard miles away. The boys—all of them—would have to help during this critical period. Learning to share the chores, such as mending nets, carrying water, and cleaning out the boats, would make the tasks much easier. Yes, soon, James and John began to recognize the advantage of having two more helping hands to aid with the heavy workloads. Bonding with Simon and Andrew grew with each passing day, and soon they became a blended family.

Poor Andrew sometimes felt like he drew the short straw much too often. He was the quiet one with his quiet smarts; however, he believed that he was always the fourth man out in all the games and work as well. It was always Andrew go fetch this or untangle that or do this other thing next. He thought his mother wrongly named him Andrew— Gopher or Ox would have fit better.

While Andrew leaned more toward learning, Simon was more interested in the village women and being out fishing when not. In between the work schedule, Salome tried her best to catch the brother's up on their lack of Jewish teachings. The boys were becoming men, and men could be easily tempted. She was also aware of the talk about that one woman over in Magdala, a Mary somebody.

Andrew became so taken with the study of the Torah that he thought he would like to work at the temple in Jerusalem, perhaps as a scribe. He enjoyed going to Jerusalem with John when they delivered fish to the authorities in the Sanhedrin. He took pleasure in looking at their fine clothes and noted how the townsmen respected them when they appeared in public.

The men of the Sanhedrin came from the affluent sections of society. Their members mainly belonged to the high-priestly class, that of the elders and the scribes. These would sit in judgment against anyone who had broken the Levitical law. Selling fish to them was constantly difficult because they always wanted more for nothing. But John was the bargainer. They soon learned that John meant what he said and remained firm on the price. Take it or leave, so take it they did.

On one particular delivery trip to Jerusalem, John asked Andrew to help again. He planned on visiting the palace house of Herod Antipas. Andrew had heard of Herodias, Herod's wife, and her beautiful daughter, so he didn't mind being the "help me and could you do this and that" errand boy that day. He listened to the scuttle-butt from the servants about a man who was dressed in camel's hair and had apparently upset their beloved Herodias. She had a temper fit and even beat a few servants over nothing. According to gossip, she was *no* saint, for she had inherited her ruthlessness from her grandfather, Herod the Great. Her marriage to Herod Antipas, Tetrarch of Galilee, was a scandalous union.

When John and Andrew arrived in this bustling city, Andrew noticed a servant girl, fair and slender, shopping at the open market. She looked up and smiled, and he smiled back in passing. Interesting thought the mesmerized Andrew, lost in her beauty. John noticed the looks that passed between the two and knew he had better quickly draw Andrew back to reality, which took addressing him twice. "Andrew. Andrew, do you hear me? Meet me back here when you are through delivering the fish to Mara Chin. We need to pick up some supplies for Susanna and the other women."

Old Mara Chin was the head cook at the palace and would be waiting for his order of fresh fish. He always picked out the fish that he wanted and would put them into his own special white pan. If the fish didn't meet his approval, he would pucker his lips and with a nod of his head, slap them back into the water container. If he approved, he would put the money into Andrew's hand, slowly bow, and briskly walk back toward his kitchen. Today, the catch would be the best, for they came right from the night's haul— beauties from the Sea of Galilee. It had been a good night's work for John and Andrew, tiring but fulfilling. They had only had a few winks of sleep. Just thinking about the customers wanting the fish to be fresh and alive revived them.

Andrew arrived at the house and knocked on the servant's entrance door, expecting to meet Mara Chin with his white pan. The door opened and—it was her! "Well, hello fish peddler, what do we have here?" she teased.

"Uhh, my lady, fish, my name is fish—uh, Andrew, my name is Andrew," he stammered, wishing he were dead when he stammered out that ridiculous statement. Now she was staring at him so hard that he stepped back down and focused his eyes away from her and back on the fish.

Lesia, recognizing the tongue slip, just decided to act like it didn't faze her although she surely wished she could have let out a big burst of laughter. She cleared her thoughts then said, "My name is Lesia. So fish peddler, Andrew, do you have Mara Chin's order?" "Yes, I just need to lift it out so you can see it." He lifted out the special water bucket container, which was very heavy. He had loaded it earlier that way, and now he so hoped that all the fish had survived the journey. Lesia was beautiful indeed, and it was all Andrew could do to keep his mind on the bucket of fish. *Would she know what fish to keep and what not?* he wondered.

He lifted the bucket up and took two steps closer to her as if in slow motion. His hand shook just as he lifted the lid. She in her quiet, lovely manner reached out to help him. Her hair fell loosely forward as she bent over to examine the fish. He hadn't expected that and wasn't ready for what was about to happen.

Lesia was inexperienced around fish, not knowing what to expect. A fish that is crowded in with other fish, a fish that is alive, a fish that is large and strong with a powerful tail—look out. Andrew felt the load shifting. "Oh, *no*, woman." One fish jumped and fell back into the pail, and with its tail flopping, the splashing water sprayed up and into Lesia's face. Her scream startled him. The water bucket lurched, and when he tried to catch it, he lost his footing and fell backward onto the bottom of the step, dumping the water and the fish on his head.

"My good, fumble fingers, fish peddler, *sir*." She couldn't finish because of her laughter. It was a beautiful, musical laughter that spilled over onto him. Then they both lost it, for hysteria had set in as they looked at each other, at the flopping fish, at her wet hair, and at his wet attire. They looked like a couple of drowned rats.

Mara Chin came running. When he saw his order on the ground, he began grabbing the flopping fish, trying to plop them into the balance of what was left in the water container. Oh, yes, here was one he wouldn't take, and shaking his head, he plopped it down right at Andrew's wet sandals. Still not looking very happy, he noticed Andrew's attire and his humble position and Lesia's wet face and hair. He had to laugh in spite of himself. "No pay, today," and chuckling, he walked briskly as always toward his kitchen.

Andrew was still on the ground looking up at Lesia, who had now calmed down. Lesia stepped down to help Andrew up. "I'm so sorry. I helped in creating this, but when you said fresh and alive, you really meant it," she quipped. Laughter rose up again at the thought of the quandary that this six foot, two inch stinky, wet, fisherman peddler had gotten himself into. He tried to explain to her how he and his friends were blessed with a nice night of fishing, the hurry to the city with a good order especially for Mara Chin, and now *this*.

She eyed him carefully and teased, "Do you smile at all the ladies in the market?" "No, my lady, just the beautiful, wet ones."

Lesia was attracted to Andrew right from the first sight of his captivating smile in the marketplace. She didn't know he was going to be the one who would stop her heart and soul. In laughter and tears, love was being born— right in the middle of a fish buying expedition. It was real. She knew it, but for now, she would hide it in her heart.

The fish buying expeditions became more frequent. Her smile would always greet him, and, of course, he smiled back. This always broke up the dull routine of just fishing and fishing. He would get lost in her smiling eyes, and he would miss some of what she was telling him about the events going on in the household, the good and the bad. Yes, he certainly enjoyed this new adventure.

3

John the Baptist

John the Baptist preached far from the temple precinct and the Holy City of Jerusalem. His message was "Repent of your sins and turn to God, for the Kingdom of Heaven is near" (Matt. 3:2). John baptized his followers to signify that their old life was gone and that they were emerging into a new life. The Jordan River was the special meeting place for Andrew and those who followed and believed this message.

Andrew wanted to go and hear John the Baptist's sermons. He needed a break from fishing. But getting away from Simon and the fishing chores was always a challenge. Thanks to John of Thunder, who helped pull the extra load in times past, Andrew was able to get away and hear John the Baptist from time to time. Maybe tomorrow John would help again.

Andrew grew to love hearing this message, and his heart was filled with great faith. "Chasing after a man in camel's hair and not a fair maiden, Andrew, what's up with this?" Simon would question. Little did they know that Salome's teaching about their heritage from Abraham, about Jews and Gentiles and mixed marriages, would be in play in both their lives.

The sweet servant girl also was growing in Andrew's mind. The upbeat manner of her speech and her smile stopped his heart every time. He wrestled within himself about thoughts of her in his life. Why *not?* Why would it matter? If David and Solomon could handle the challenge of many wives, couldn't he handle just one? He thought about Simon's marriage and about how the hardship of fishing had left Anna alone much of the time. He remembered the time he helped Anna with her only birth. *Could I put a wife through this same mold?* he wondered. *Could I, a Galilean, with my speech and looks, take a wife? A servant girl with mixed lineage. Would my Zebedee family accept this marriage?* Since Anna was part Jewish, Simon had that in his favor before going into his marriage. But if Salome objected, it would break his heart because she had become his mother, and her opinions meant a great deal to him.

Lesia was fluent in Italian as well as in her native tongue. She had an elegant way about her and a stylishness that she carried with her every day. Would she be able to clean and cook fish, bathe babies, and mend fishing nets while waiting out storms when her husband didn't make it home? But then, he knew she was as beautiful inside as she was on the outside. This didn't make his decision any easier as she was a maidservant to the queen, a queen with a reputation. She could easily attract Herodias's anger, and the queen could have her killed. Old hateful. Andrew's quiet ways fit his demeanor, but with the weight of love growing, his insides became a tumbling volcano.

4

Following Jesus

The day came—a day that would change Andrew's life forever. Jesus, the Lamb of God, appeared at the Jordan shoreline and was baptized by John the Baptist.

When Jesus was raised out of the water, Andrew heard a voice sounding out of the sky and saw a dove appear and cover Jesus's right shoulder. Wow! Believing in his head and now knowing in his heart, this Jesus truly was the long awaited Messiah. He knew he must tell Simon and the others.

Andrew was with Simon, James, and John the day Jesus appeared at the Galilee seashore and spoke to them saying, "Come, follow me, and I will show you how to fish for people!" (Matt. 4:19). This was the beginning of change for the Sons of Thunder, Andrew, and his big brother Simon.

In the home of Salome and James Zebedee, there was a void. As they began their evening meal together, they felt the loneliness of the empty chairs, chairs belonging to their boys. Zeb prepared to read from the Torah. Salome sat quietly and said, "Salome, my name means 'God has given'; now God has taken away." As Salome covered her head and sang the Sabbath song, she lit the candle on the beautiful table as she did time and time before. Zeb began to read from the selected passage for this Sabbath evening, a passage out of Isaiah.

Nevertheless, that time of darkness and despair will not go on forever. The land of Zebulun and Naphtali will be humbled, but there will be a time in the future when Galilee of the Gentiles, which lies along the road that runs between the Jordan and the sea, will be filled with glory. The people who walk in darkness will see a great light. For those who live in a land of deep darkness, a light will shine. For a child is born to us, a son is given to us. The government will rest on his shoulders. And he will be called: Wonderful Counselor, Mighty God, Everlasting Father, Prince of Peace. His government and its peace will never end. He will rule with fairness and justice from the throne of his ancestor David for all eternity.

The passionate commitment of the LORD of Heaven's Armies will make this happen! (Isa. 9:1-2, 6-7).

Both, bowing their heads, now knew that this Jesus who was walking on their land and property preaching the "kingdom is at hand" was the Son given to the world, and He had chosen their children for His kingdom.

Kissing Salome on her forehead, Zeb began to comfort her with, "We've experienced something that many parents haven't. We now willingly give our children to God knowing that He will take care of them. I have always wanted to have children in the temple service. Yes, and tomorrow I will go to the other villages and hire some young men to help replace the boys. I have forty villages to choose from, Salome, so don't worry, our fishing business will not suffer."

"Yes." She smiled sweetly.

With the peace of God in their hearts, they prepared for the night. Zebedee's sleep was pleasant and peaceful. While Salome lay beside him, she thought about the kingdom. Could her sons be kings? Could they sit by His side? She too drifted off to sleep, a sleep that was sweet and restful.

5

The Teachings of Jesus

One day as Jesus was teaching near Tiberias, great crowds assembled to hear Him. His disciples told Jesus to send the people away because they needed food.

But Andrew called Jesus's attention to a lad who had five barley loaves and two fishes. Jesus looked to heaven, blessed the loaves and fishes, and fed the multitudes. Having begun as a disciple of John the Baptist, Andrew now continued in ministry with Jesus both before and after John's death.

The rulers in John the Baptist's generation did not accept him, alleging instead that he was demon possessed as was later said of Jesus himself. John was beheaded in AD 29 by the Tetrarch Herod Antipas, who had married his brother's wife, Herodias. Herod was grieved at being required to execute John but had given his oath before witnesses to Herodias' daughter, Salome, because of his pleasure in her dance. Andrew knew that danger was in the air for certain after that event.

A highlight of Andrew's time with Jesus was the day when they were there on the Mount of Olives. Jesus had explained about the destruction of the temple. Andrew asked Jesus privately, "Tell us, when will this happen, and what will be the sign of your coming and of the end of the age?" (Matt. 24:3).

Jesus answered, "Don't let anyone mislead you, for many will come in my name, claiming, 'I am the Messiah.' They will deceive many. And you will hear of wars and threats of wars, but don't panic. Yes, these things must take place, but the end won't follow immediately. Nation will go to war against nation, and kingdom against kingdom. There will be famines and earthquakes in many parts of the world. But all this is only the first of the birth pains, with more to come" (Matt. 24:4-8). He told all of them about the persecutions they would suffer and that only those who endured to the end would be saved.

Jesus told about the suffering such as had not been from the beginning of creation. He explained that after the suffering, the Son of Man would come in the clouds with great power and glory, and only the Father knew the time of the Son's return. "I say to all, keep awake!" Jesus commanded. "The doorkeeper must be on watch."

6

The Pierced Ear

In the final year of His ministry, Jesus went up to Jerusalem for a feast of the Jews. Entering in by the Sheep Gate, going through one of the five covered colonnades, He came to the pool of Bethesda. Here a great number of disabled lay: the blind, the lame, the paralyzed. There He found a man who had been sick all his life. Jesus asked him, "Would you like to get well?" (John 5:6). Jesus told him to rise, take up his bed, and walk. And He did!

When the Jewish leaders saw that the man was healed and carried his bed, they objected because it was the Sabbath. They said to the man, "You can't work on the Sabbath! The law doesn't allow you to carry that sleeping mat!" (John 5:10). This made the leaders angry and more determined to persecute Jesus. Meanwhile, Jesus opened up scriptures to the people. "I assure you, those who listen to my message and believe in God who sent me have eternal life. They will never be condemned for their sins, but they have already passed from death into life" (John 5:24).

Seeing that Jesus was very busy, Andrew seized this opportunity for himself, shared his plan with Philip, and then quietly slipped away. As he did this, his mind drew him to another place—that of the lovely woman, Lesia. She needed to know why he had not been around to see her. He knew she would be perplexed as to what happened to him and the others. She had to know today that he really cared for her. More than that, she had to know how much he cared for Jesus as well. He was one of Jesus's disciples. Jesus had kept all twelve of his disciples very close to Him. Andrew always felt like he was the fourth one out, so he didn't think that Jesus would miss him if he took a little time to see Lesia. Just in case, Philip would cover for him.

Andrew's thoughts were on the one chance to again see the loveliest angel he had ever known. With anticipation, he arrived at her door and knocked. As kindred hearts go, Lesia heard the knock and knew immediately that it was Andrew.

When the door opened, a vision of loveliness appeared before Andrew. Lesia's hair was down and flowing, half obscuring the openness of her right shoulder in her Roman tunica, a tunica to die for with it silkiness and colorful pattern. Yes, a very striking appearance, this expensive gown no man—if in his right mind—would ignore. She welcomed him in with her smile and twirled her floating hair again, exposing now her open shoulder and the tightness of the Roman fit along the waist.

The gossip of the household flowed freely from her. She began with the dance that Herodias's daughter did and how the head of John the Baptist, that man from the desert, had been brought right into the central dining hall on a platter. She spoke of tiptoeing around the depressed Herod and of the haughtiness and smugness of Herodias. She gestured and twirled to show even more of the drama for Andrew to fully understand. Yes, Andrew was not missing a thing.

Lesia told Andrew how Salome, that terrible daughter, just like her mother, had run screaming from the palace hall and had cried in her room for days because of her mother's request, like she didn't understand the part she had played in that horrible deed. Now Herodias, fearing the Jesus movement, had decided that they would have to leave for Rome on the morrow.

"The darling little dancer needs a change, Herodias told me. Running away is her answer to the situation, and so she has barked out her orders like a mad woman."

"I don't want to go, Andrew. I don't want to leave. I, I…" The sadness of the last statement came also with tears flowing freely down her soft, tender face as she repeated the wail of her eminent departure, having to go when she didn't want to. "Mara Chin won't go against the madness of Herodias, fearing for his own neck."

Andrew touched her soft, silk tunica and stroked her right arm and her open shoulder, all the while adjusting his own thoughts and heart to what he was hearing. Finally, he placed his hands around Lesia's face and lifted it up toward him. He felt each tear on his calloused hands. He brushed back her hair on one side and then the other side, kissing the trembling maiden as he held her close and began to whisper, "It's all right," even though he knew it wasn't. Now because of the news of her leaving, he knew that he must tell her today, right now, to really tell her of his growing affections: his love for her as well as his love for Jesus.

It was then he noticed her ear—her earlobe with its lobe piece, which had the ring of the servant-for-life tightly embedded, embedded by the pounding of the hammer on the special slave-for-life metal ring. Her ear had been pierced. The teaching from Deuteronomy came to his mind. Soul sickness hit inside of him. He realized that Lesia was a slave for life because of the lifetime servant covenant made in the household of Herod, made with the hard-hearted Herodias.

Andrew quietly thought, *Would this woman who hated Jews and had no respect for their laws, their beliefs, set my beloved free? Never!* Andrew's heart folded up like hearing the T'qiah, the moaning sound of the Hebrew ram's horn, the shofar, wailing—wailing, long and sadly. His heart receded and closed out the sound, placing it into a soundless case. Would love ever play again for him?

He swallowed hard and held back his tears. Yes, the manly thing to do was to comfort the maiden. Then he sighed and forced himself to smile and drew her into his arms for a comforting hug for himself as well as for his love. He then began to tell her about Jesus and about His kingdom. He told her that since John the Baptist had died, Jesus had now become more open about what He was doing and what He was teaching. Andrew was unaware of himself going on and on and on and on.

He kissed her again as she brushed back a lock away from his ear and remarked, "Hearing your heart for this Jesus, I believe that your ear now wears an unseen earring. You are His slave," she commented as she continued to tug at his ear.

Andrew suddenly found himself growing quiet. Inside his spirit, she had hit a nerve. He had vowed to his beloved John the Baptist and to the new kingdom a new allegiance. Allegiance to Jesus? A new loyalty was being birth within, not realized and not spoken until Lesia's touch, the soft touch and tug to his ear.

Andrew realized now that Lesia hadn't met him before her vow. He knew that providence was in play in both of their lives. Could she reach Herodias's hateful and wicked heart with the Good News? Could he be a fisher of men? Unknown to both, their hands reached up to their own ears and lingered for a moment, sensing togetherness.

Andrew realized now that she would always be his by her touch to his ear, and he would always be hers with that last kiss on her ear, each now to walk a path of singleness, each obeying his or her own master. Andrew was usually the fourth man out, hiding things in his heart. He was now vowing to be that good and faithful servant and disciple. Time would tell.

7

Lazarus

As the day was waning in Jerusalem, Jesus began the journey back to the Sea of Galilee with His disciples. Andrew fell in step silently by the side of Philip, his thoughts tucked behind his masculinity. With a sarcastic smile, Andrew voiced his musings, "Well, here we are walking behind the Master and His three pets." Philip was of Bethsaida, the city of Andrew and Peter, and knew well how the fourth man out always worked: Peter, then James and John, followed by Andrew. Philip knew that he himself was the sixth man out, considering all twelve disciples. He felt like this because of Nathanael, the man whom Jesus said had no guile. Sensing that something else was eating Andrew, he steered the conversation to memories of the last occasion when he and Andrew had visited Mary, Martha, and Lazarus.

Bethany, a tiny village on the slope of the Mount of Olives, was the home of Mary, Martha, and Lazarus. Martha was a great cook and very hospitable along with her sister Mary. Andrew remembered a conversation Martha had had with Jesus. "Lord, doesn't it seem unfair that my sister just sits here while I do all the work? Tell her to come and help me" (Luke 10:38-42). But Jesus's reply was that Martha worried about many things when only one thing was needed, and that Mary had chosen that part, which would not be taken away from her.

As they walked, Philip talked about Lazarus and all the people the Lord was healing, but Andrew's mind was miles away. The kiss and the good-bye were still burning within his bosom. Choose what is better? Mary chose what was better. His heart was heavy. "Oh my lovely one, we can't choose each other. Yes, like Mary, I choose to follow Jesus." His hand lingered longer on his ear as his mind returned to Philip and all his chatter.

It was Andrew's belief that Mary, Martha, and Lazarus were an extended family of Jesus, for it was evident that Jesus loved them. Philip, as he chattered on, wondered about Lazarus as they had enjoyed that last evening together, eating and fellowshipping with Jesus. Did Lazarus seem to look a little tired? Indeed, they agreed, he did.

Days later, the disciples found themselves back in Bethany. Lazarus was dead! What on earth had happened? Jesus had received the message from Bethany that Lazarus was ill. Yet Jesus had stayed where He was for two more days (John 11:1). Everyone wondered why they didn't head back to Bethany immediately. But Jesus's plan was all for the glory of God. When they arrived in Bethany, many had come to comfort Mary and Martha concerning their brother. Martha, seeing Jesus coming, ran to Him. "Lord, if you had been here my brother would not have died." They led Jesus to the place where Lazarus was buried. Andrew witnessed something that went beyond all human knowledge. Jesus, crying out in a loud voice, commanded, *"Lazarus, come forth!"* (John 11:43). And— Lazarus came out of the tomb! The one who was dead was now alive.

The crowds were now ten deep around Lazarus, and with tears of joy, they were praising God and kissing Lazarus along with Mary and Martha. Andrew walked back to the opening of the cave where Lazarus had been laid four days before, the grave clothes and head cloth still smelling of death lay on the ground. Yes, this was real. Andrew went a short distance and let his tears fall.

He sought God and said, "Yes, I will serve the one who created all life and has the consummation of all people and things in His hands." Placing his hands over his tearstained face, he bowed in prayer with silent reverence.

Two days before Passover, Andrew and the others with Jesus went to Bethany again before going into Jerusalem. When Passover arrived, it was a somber time with all of them in the upper room, where they heard about the new covenant. After the Passover meal, they went to the Mount of Olives to the garden of Gethsemane, where Jesus told them to sit and pray. Andrew, the fourth man out, didn't go with the inner circle—Peter, James, and John—to the special place in the garden where Jesus prayed alone. After the soldiers came, Philip and Andrew left to go back to Capernaum.

The crucifixion, the resurrection, the ascension—all now past.

8

The Disciples' Early Days

Andrew was with the other ten disciples when Jesus upbraided them for their lack of faith and stubbornness because they had not believed the report of those that had seen Jesus after He had arisen. They all heard the orders, "Go into all the world and preach the Good News to everyone. Anyone who believes and is baptized will be saved…[Many] miraculous signs will accompany those who believe…" (Mark 16:15-17).

Yes, knowing the orders was one thing but fulfilling them—that would be the challenge. For the first few days, it was sort of easy to feel like slipping back into the old fishing routine. They hadn't yet received the power that would enable them for doing the work set before them by God, let alone living it. The gift of the Comforter was not only the glue but was also the strength and power. They began to see the change right away. A holy boldness first started with Andrew's brother Peter.

Peter did a great job of preaching. He was so changed now, so on fire for the "cause of mankind." Andrew felt awed, the same awe that came upon everyone because of the many wonders and signs that followed all of them. It was a love so strong it flowed among the people. Many began to sell their possessions and goods and distribute the proceeds to all (Act 2:43). At first, it seemed that the only accomplishment was just eating and breaking bread, while the Good News Gospel kept adding to the numbers.

In addition, the sick were being healed, but stop then the tide turned (Act 4), Peter and John were speaking to the people one day when the priests, the captain of the temple, and the Sadducees came upon them (Acts 4). The Sadducees were especially annoyed because Peter and John were teaching in the name of Jesus and preaching about the resurrection of the dead, in which the authorities did not believe. So the order went out that Peter and John were to be arrested. They were brought before the rulers, who were astounded by their boldness, especially when the rulers realized that these were uneducated and ordinary men—companions of

Jesus. But because the authorities could not deny the notable miracle, the healing of the man lame from birth, they were only able to threaten Peter and John then let them go.

Peter, Andrew's muscular protector, the winner of most of the arm wrestling matches, was now not only a fisher of men but a healer of many (Acts 5). His ministry was so great that the people carried the sick out into the streets and laid them on cots and mats, in order that Peter's shadow might fall on some of them as he came by.

Time and again Peter went to prison for the Gospel. Time and again Jesus delivered him. No matter what the authorities said or did, however, Peter kept right on preaching. The death of Stephen and James's was painful, but when Peter would begin to praise with song and worship, the disciples could feel the presence of the Holy Spirit, a presence that always made the hair on their neck and arms stand up. Again when Peter was in Rome with his wife and Petronilla, he annoyed the authorities because of the power of the miraculous healings. So Peter once again found himself facing the closing of prison doors and unkind service.

9

Rome

Gaius rearranged the food tray for Simon. "Here, fisherman, looks like you live another day. The council must want to do something special with you. Maybe they want you to call on your Jesus. You say He is alive. Well, then, have Him show up and fight our gladiators," laughing and making hand gestures. "Or they might let you enter our games since you seemed to have strong arms. Perhaps they want you to go out to the games and raise the dead." Laughter again filled the small space.

"Gaius, Jesus loves you. You know He is the King of the Jews in the new world to come." Gaius just spit into the corner and turned to leave. "Has anyone else come to visit?" asked Simon softly.

"No!"

"Wait. I did hear someone say that a man named Andrew was here. They might let him in to see you." Simon felt a beat of love throb through his heart. Andrew.

The next day, Andrew entered the prison and secretly slipped Gaius a generous coin knowing from the day before that he was a greedy sort. He had figured Gaius out right away. Gaius gladly played with the coin between his fingers as he led Andrew back to see his beloved brother. They, as brothers, renewed their familial energy when they embraced as best they could between bars and chains. "Andrew, you must leave Rome. Now!" commanded Simon.

Andrew reached down through those bars taking hold of Simon's chain hand and while holding it said "The same old big brother act. Okay, I will." But the thoughts that were wandering inside his head were not of leaving but going and trying to see his Lesia. *Got to see her before I leave. I must*, he thought.

"Simon, God has not shown me what to do, and if I leave, which way? North? South?

I've just been asking God where I should go. I feel lost right now, dear brother."

Hidden underneath was a slowly growing frustration with his calling. In addition, his longed for Lesia, whom he had never forgotten even when he knew it was futile to continue to pine for her. He had to come to reality. The commandment, "Go," was heard and understood, but it still lingered in silence over him.

"Andrew, look at me. You know all things are in His time and will. He will show you. Keep your faith and trust. Keep remembering the big picture—God's love for mankind." Peter slips him a note which read: Catacombs. Brown door.

"Enough you two," growled Gaius, shoving Andrew. "You've got to go now. Here, go this back way and be quiet." He then acted like he would reconsider Andrew staying awhile longer.

The big, ungrateful bully, thought Andrew. "Bet he wants another generous offer, but not this time, soldier boy," Andrew growled under his breath as he turned to leave. Going through the door, he had to put his hands over his eyes from the shock of the sunlight in the busy street.

Simon, meanwhile, headed to his corner, where he began to whisper intercessory prayers for all Christians. Gaius just shook his head as he retrieved the tray and again checked his pocket, feeling the generous tip from Andrew.

Andrew, while reading the note again, looked in all the directions to determine which way he and his newly purchased little donkey should go. "Let's see, Malka, we have to go toward the outskirts of the city, toward the burial ground. Here, let's see which road," he muttered. He looked up at the words: Via Appia, then Via Ostiense, then Via Tiburtina. "Let's stop and take a moment, girl," even though Malka was pulling toward the right road and the tug was shifting her load.

He didn't know which road to take. If only Gaius had given him more time with Simon. He had wanted to ask more about the directions, but that guard was too close for comfort, and if he had heard, then a calamity would have occurred, and it would have been his fault for trying to get more directions. "So, Malka, my faithful companion, it is up to us to do this alone. Here, let me readjust your load, and then we will go."

"I still can't believe that Simon is in jail, Malka. The cell was so smelly, small, and poorly lit. Simon is used to fresh air and sunlight. He always took great pleasure in the waves of the Sea of Galilee, but now he is penned up like some animal."

"I hope we can find this place, Malka. While her ear twitched again looking at the wadded up note, he reread the small scribbled message. "Okay. Brown door, brown door. What does that mean, and what does it look like?" His mind went into his skill of logic filtering. Brown not blue, ok sky this rules you out, smiling, now you tree and rocks, hmmmmm, brown, ground. He was constantly talking to himself.

He had heard from the townspeople that the catacombs here in Rome provided protection for people and were used for ceremonies and displaying Christian symbols. They have countless chambers that line the tunnels from what they tell me.

Simon wanted him to go check on Anna and Petronilla, who were hiding out there, but again, he knew that he should act with some kind of caution. He decided to play the nonchalant traveler with donkey. "Okay, Malka, you can play along as well." He laughed at this amusing image, but then a serious moment penetrated the evening air. The aura of politics and the changing of kings and governments seemed to surround and overhang the city. Life was becoming more perilous with the specter of persecutions and death looming ever larger. The division of beliefs silently spoke to him as his feet walked toward the soft volcanic tufo rock under Rome's ***catacombs.

"Brown door? There isn't any door. It looks like a person enters by stooping or stepping over or stepping down." Slowly, he approached a series of narrow steps when a man with a cane drew near.

"Good evening, traveler. How is it with you?"

"Well, kind friend, I am looking for a brown door to go into, but to my surprise, I see none."

"Yes," said the stranger. "Who are you, may I ask?"

"Oh, my name is Andrew, and my donkey is Malka. We were at the prison today, and Simon, my brother, gave me a message to come here and look for a brown door. I guess I should have taken the Via Ostiense road instead."

"Oh, no," said the stranger. "You have a code, and if you please follow me, you shall find the rest of Simon's family safe and enjoying a peaceful meal." They descended down several layers of steps, and turning right, he lit a torch from the side of the wall and led the way.

The chambers widened, and they entered another larger room. The smell of food was wonderful, and he then remembered that he hadn't eaten. Anna, when she saw him, made a mad dash toward him. "Andrew, you came. Oh, bless the God of Abraham. Did you see Simon, did you?"

They ate. Then they remained awake to talk and sort out the events that lead them to where they were, sitting here in the catacombs, hiding so that they would not be killed, so that the commission from Jesus would be fulfilled. Soon the night was spent.

The next morning, Aquila led him back out of the chamber, and they retraced their steps up the narrow passage called the brown door. "Hey, little lady, queen Malka, are you ready to go?" And of course, he continued talking to her.

"Simon really found a great jewel in Anna as a companion. She loves winning people to the cause of Jesus as much as Simon does. She has known tragedy, but she knows that the kingdom is the best portion of her life along with her family. Putting up with Simon and his snoring was always her cross to bear, Malka." He reached over and stroked the donkey's nose. Chuckling, "You know, Malka, Anna was a godsend to me and that brother of mine when I lived with them. She was a very good cook and got after us about cleaning, especially after the fishing loads. She always pulled her weight, just like the other women in Galilee, especially Salome Zebedee, who set a good example for us all.

He touched the package all wrapped up nice and tightly and already hanging on the side of his saddle. "Little queen, I'm glad you were a good donkey and didn't run away. Did Anna give you a hug, too?" Andrew went back in time remembering when Salome also knew when to hug him when the three mischievous boys, Simon, James, and John, would pick on him and pin his arms down—three against one, pulling his arms down then calling him a loser. "Malka, I remember yelling, 'See, it takes the three of you guys to match me,' and then I would run. I really wouldn't care if they were doing that right now. I miss them, and I miss Lesia. I miss Salome and Zeb, too. They were a big part of my life. Now I miss Philip, the rest of the disciples, and Jesus."

He remembered that if he headed north he would be passing the Market Place again. He tugged on Malka so that she would know to turn back toward Rome. "Yes, little queen, I almost forgot that I do need some important things, so let's stop and get them. Okay, girl?"

Neighing, Malka sounded like she was saying, "Okay."

"I also have not seen Lesia and that is the most important purpose I have in going in this direction, a purpose that nobody else knows about. I really would like to see her. I feel she needs to tell me something, something I really want to hear."

Neighing and nodding her head, little queen Malka seemed to say, "That's the way, lover boy. Andrew, let's go." He looked at Malka but didn't say anything. Malka was thinking about what her ears were doing, a slow twitching of the right ear, which shortly would increase into the full God-sky, a secret that would be in place for Andrew.

He was walking around the market softly whispering, "Lord, now what," when realization set in. "I am leaving. I just said good-bye to Anna and the family. But I haven't seen *her*. Lord, I feel so lost." A tear dropped as he touched his ear, the only point of contact that his heart and soul sensed inside. The closest thing that reminded him of *her* was remembering her touch on his ear.

Walking into the leather booth, he purchased a pair of sandals and decided to wear them right away. Speaking to his feet and new sandals, he remarked, "You better last and make walking easier for what you just cost me! Did I just hear little queen neigh?"

Then—there she was—Lesia, with her full basket over her arm. She was now looking intensely at a necklace or ring or something at the jewelry booth. *Why*—his thoughts raced—*I could go right now and grab her and throw her on my donkey and be gone before old Hateful misses her.* His thoughts were jarred by the loud commotion of four Roman soldiers marching hurriedly, herding and shoving a group of Christians toward the prison area.

Whew! he thought. *I'm glad I didn't try that. Getting me killed is one thing, but her— never.* He chose for now to drink in her beauty from where he was standing, like a bee drinks in the nectar from a lovely flower. She turned once his way then paused with her heavy load and headed for home.

Herodias snapped in a snobbish tone toward Lesia as she entered the dressing room. "Did you get what I wanted? Nero is having quite a garden party tonight, and I want to look special," she commented as she admired herself in her long obsidian polish stone mirrors.

"Yes," Lesia gasped as her breath returned once again after the long walk. Noticing Lesia's demeanor, Herodias said, "What's wrong?"

"I felt like someone's eyes were on me in the market place today." Inside she felt a presence of someone, like when Andrew came to bring the fish. *Hateful, woman. Why does she always pick my brain,* Lesia thought, not daring to speak aloud.

"If you're still mourning over that young fisherman, I hoping Nero does away with them all! Forget him. We're in Rome. *Forget him.*" Herodias had a spiteful attitude.

Heading down the hall, Lesia faced the wall so if another servant was about he or she wouldn't see the hurtful expression on her face or see her crying. Dropping to her knees, holding her earring, she whispered, "Forget you, Andrew, my soul mate—never! Never! I will love you to the end."

*** underground burial places

10

Praying for Guidance

Malka walked along beside Andrew and was almost in step with him as he talked to her, almost like she was a human companion. "Yes, the bread and the wine will taste good later tonight."

Malka neighed and shook her head sideways, thinking, *For you maybe, but not for me.*

Donkeys don't like wine. Oats for me would taste good later tonight.

He continued to talk to her as though she were his walking partner, Philip. "I just heard about the big celebrations and their bloody games coming up in Rome. But I feel in my heart of hearts that Simon will be released soon. It is a very corrupt city, and Simon has a burden for these people. Lord, help Simon. Malka, my good donkey, may God help Rome."

The walk felt good, and Malka was a pleasant one for a donkey. Andrew gave thanks for this small favor. The night was closing in fast, and the full moon was now above his head. He stopped by a small stream for the night, hoping that a good breakfast of fish would be for the taking in the morning's light. While the fire was taking hold, he turned to Malka, "You did alright today carrying me even with my long legs, huh." He smiled, gave her a good handful of oats, and covered her back with one of his old blankets.

Rearranging his own bedding around the glowing fire, he reached down to untie the straps of his new sandals. Thoughts were many and coming fast as he gazed into the flickering flames of the fire. It's funny how memories mix with the wind and darkness of the night: Jerusalem, Mara Chin with his white pan, Jesus, his and Simon's early childhood, the persecutions that were starting in Rome.

His mind then turned to a most precious memory—Lesia, the sweetest maiden of all, the one who had stolen his heart. It was comforting to remember the soft touch of her hand moving back his hair, teasing him about his unknown call, and pulling on his ear lobe saying, "You are a slave, too."

And, yes, other memories: that final Passover dinner when Jesus had washed all their feet, the seriousness of the Master, and the quietness that fell on all of them when Judas exited the room hurriedly. After Jesus had washed Simon Peter's feet, He came to Andrew. Jesus had looked him right in the eyes. Andrew had felt then that Jesus was going to say something to him about what he should do, but He didn't. Then other events followed quickly: the arrest, trial, and ultimately, the joy of seeing Jesus again until He ascended into the awaiting clouds.

"Now, dear Simon is in jail, and I am here alone, going where?" His troubling thoughts then began to mingle into his mind like the many night noises. His thoughts were drifting out into the dark, big open space of shelter, the open arena with only the fire and his beautiful queen, the donkey, for comfort. What did Jesus say about thoughts? He must not let troubling doubt take hold, not now. Sighing and staring out into the openness, he remembered that Jesus would slip away and go to pray to His Father in secret. "Pray, I must do, too."

Placing his head into his hands, Andrew began praying, "Jesus, your sayings are strong upon my heart tonight. Directions, guidance are needed. Please, dear Jesus, Master. He that endures to the end will be saved. Anna, Salome, James and John—God, love and remember my family and loving friends. Amen."

Andrew placed his head down to sleep and pulled the blanket tightly as the moon continued shimmering upon the water as a soft breeze wafted, moving now among the trees. Yes, Jesus did have something for Andrew. Tonight it would come. It would come as the music of countries that Jesus wanted Andrew to visit with the Good News. It would come as notes of the bagpipe, lyre, Turkic drum, bandura, lute, and kobza. Yes, called to places that were like him, a man on the outside.

In the morning, Malka would also become part of the Good News team that Andrew didn't even understand yet. It is when the Sovereign Kingdom of Yeshua Keeps you and His Handiwork (Psalm 19) (Isaiah 40). A love package that God sets up with the creatures He created, unseen to the human eye.

11

Malka and the Angel

Malka felt the dew under her legs and proceeded to arise and stretch as all donkeys do. She kept hearing Andrew during the night. It sounded like he was singing and preaching and then humming. She was sure most humans did this, but last night Andrew was especially expressive.

Then she saw the Angel. He was standing by the stream and came over to the fire where the coals had cooled down. She moved around the tree so he wouldn't see her but then remembered her mother's words about the secret that belonged only to their family.

"Good morning, little one. We meet again," the angel called.

"Yes," Malka neighed. "You were there in Jerusalem the night I was born in the house of Nicodemus."

"I see that the servant lineage is still present in you as it was in your great-great- grandfather's time. (2 Peter 2:16) Grandfather Adara (noble) was so careful carrying Mother Mary to Bethlehem."

"Yes, Joseph loved Adara and was glad that he had that noble donkey when he left during the night to flee to Egypt with the baby Jesus."

God, the Father, had equipped Adara with a good set of nighttime eyes, so the escape from the town was a success. By the time they were leaving, the soldiers were already sneaking into Bethlehem, spying out the townspeople for King Herod, especially the women, in search for baby boys ages one to three. Grandmother Damara with Aliza (joyful), who was young at the time, walked alongside *Him* and Marni into the city of Jerusalem, while the people were spreading palm branches and singing Hosanna to the King. Nathaniel, one of the disciples, told Nicodemus that the Lord had need of them. Grandmother Marni (rejoice) had a servant's heart, as well. Later, Marni told Malka's mother, Aliza, who was just a colt at the time, that Jesus had touched her young ears and patted her head.

The secret of the blessing of Adara began with baby Jesus and, yet today, continues to come down through their lineage. From that time on, they could understand humans. In addition, her mother's right ear twitched a little faster than most donkeys and would begin to softly glow whenever she was involved in a special mission.

Nicodemus loved riding grandmother Marni even though he had money enough to buy a fine horse. Aliza had spoken to Nicodemus about Malka through her special ear twitching, telling him that Malka was to be sent to Rome for a special God enlightening

S.K.Y. job that would take her to many other countries and many cities. Her ears would help attract children so they could receive a blessing. That was what Jesus wanted—for little children to come to Him so He could do what He loved to do most and that would be to bless them. Now she was blessed to be Andrew's beast of burden.

"I am so grateful now, but when I was sold, I felt like I wasn't good enough, sort of a donkey reject, small in height and with a twitching ear," Malka told the Angel. The Angel reached over and patted her head and her ears. Suddenly, her eyes were opened, and she became aware that this was no ordinary Angel. It was *Him*.

12

Sent by God to Unknown Strangers

The sun arose in the east and began to penetrate among the leaves. It hit Andrew's face as it awakened him. Stretching, as he began to stand, his eyes fastened on the fish that was slowing spinning on the spindle over the last embers of the fire, embers that should have been too cool for cooking. How? What? Where? He turned every which way, but, no, Jesus wasn't here in His physical body. But? The fish? At that last breakfast on the shore of Galilee, Jesus had fixed breakfast. But now? It couldn't be, could it?

Then he bent down to the ground and worshipped Jesus, the savior of all mankind. The Jesus who loves. The Jesus who does miracles. The Jesus who had filled his heart all night long with the music of European countries. The Jesus who hears and answers prayers. The Jesus who now had all of him. The Jesus who had fixed his breakfast that morning. His ear was pierced for life.

Happiness was beyond description; joy was too large to describe. All he could do was praise God, eat his food, and hug Malka. It was time to break camp. "Yes, my big brother, I see the bigger picture. God, please wrap your arms around Simon as he faces solitude in that prison in Rome and keep Anna safe."

"Let's go, girl. We've got some preaching to do."

He led Malka along beside him, still licking his fingers from that tasty breakfast of fish and all the while smiling, crying, and laughing. He was hopping and skipping as well. Only God knew what all this tall fourth man out did now that Andrew knew what his calling was. His heart would never turn back. Never! Did Malka just do a skip? Did she see something?

The fish gave him the energy to continue the trip north. The beauty of the Black Sea and the small villages of lovely people stood before him. The people were strangers by tongue, but when Andrew sketched pictures, the people seemed to understand the Good News message. Some wanted more and enjoyed hearing about the miracles, stories about the blind and how they were healed. Better still when Andrew laid hands on them and healings were manifested, believers were born.

Andrew now knew the reason for the "eye-on" teaching from John the Baptist and his Messiah, Jesus. He knew he would not be just another voice of a fourth man out, but in his heart, he would be first with his commission. He vowed again as he touched his ear. He had left his boats, his own personal life, and had answered the call. Yes, he had heard the call. Now he was sure.

Traveling would be long and dangerous; however, over the months, years—every day—in the middle of his own crises and discouragements or in the midst of the problems of others, he would just touch his slave ear and remember his beloved Master. The Spirit would refill him and strength would always be there. The Spirit would play the music of the call and the birth of the beautiful vision. This would take him through bad weather and hungry days and lonely nights. It took him through times when people loved him and through towns that hated him and threw him out. It took him through the sharing of grief, death, and weddings with many people who, like him, were on the outside or outskirts, so to speak.

13

The Borysthenes River

Andrew and Malka left the village of Bil's'ke northeast of the big river and kept heading south, stopping wherever they found anyone or any groups of settlers who were trying to eke out a new existence for themselves. If the Good News was received, many times others in the area would not welcome them. Then Andrew would shake his sandals and on they would go.

On this day, Andrew was intent on getting back to Oibia. They were just nearing the town of Kamians'ke, located by Borysthenes River, when it became evident that something was going on in this little town. Yet how to tell Andrew? Andrew's head kept him heading south toward Oibia; then he wanted to go on to Tiras. Finally, as they came to the outskirts of the town, they stopped for lunch on the banks of the river. After eating, Andrew again turned toward the south. Then and only then did Malka react.

Malka neighed and neighed and neighed. Andrew turned, saying loudly, "What's wrong? What's up, Malka?" So—she gave him an answer. She jerked her head really hard and reared right up like any good, stubborn mule would do. She balked again, and then with her head lowered, she pushed Andrew.

"No, Malka, don't shove me. Malka, don't, not into the river." But over into the river he went. Never fear, Andrew could swim like a fish, but nevertheless, the shock of the coolness of the water and its depth did frighten even him. He came up sputtering and yelling at Malka and said, "What has gotten into you?" At that, she left him and headed down the rough, dirt road toward the little town.

Will he follow? thought Malka. *Yes, I can hear him. I think he has gotten better at expressing his thoughts. James and John would be proud.*

Entering the little town, Malka, with her attuned ears following the sounds, found herself outside of a small hut. Inside the hut, a mother was wiping three small children's foreheads with cold compresses, doing the best she knew how with no medical supplies. She hummed a nervous little tune to try and sooth the children, who were all hot with fever.

Andrew, who had kept on following, glared hard in Malka's direction with a "wait until I get to you" kind of look. Just as he caught up with her at the small hut, the mother of the children stepped outside and was startled to see Andrew, a stranger, so close to her hut. She didn't understand his greeting or his dress or that donkey—Andrew with his wet attire and unkempt hair, the donkey with her twitching right ear, which was beginning to glow. Only she couldn't see the glow with her human eye.

Andrew pulled from his saddle bag, his manuscripts and scrolls and began to show her some sketches. It was then that all three children began to cry, and Andrew asked through his sketches if he could help. The mother hesitated, but then Andrew had the look of a saint on his face now, so she stepped aside and let him enter. He looked at the small room, the poorest of the poor he thought. Now he knew that God does lead by other means than just through his brain. "Thanks, Malka," he indicated with a smile, flashing an all is forgiven signal to his donkey. Then startled, Andrew wondered, *Did Malka just wink her eye at me?*

Andrew knelt down by each one of the children, and with his right hand on their forehead and with the other hand lifted to the God of heaven; he prayed a prayer in the name of Jesus, the living Christ, and the Savior of mankind. Within minutes, all three children were begging for food. Andrew remembered the five thousand who were fed. He went to the saddle bag and returned with a few dried fish and cheese. Closing his eyes for just that sweet moment, he could remember the twelve baskets of leftovers that he and the others picked up after Jesus prayed. Remembering that Jesus blessed the fishes and loaves, he lifted up the small bundle with his right hand as he closed his eyes. Then opening it like Jesus did and looking upward, he said, "Thank you, God." Everyone ate until each was filled. Healing, happiness, and the presence of the message of the Good News permeated the air.

The whole town heard the Good News of the Gospel, and of course, Malka was the star of the town with all the children. She let her ear twitch and glow now for all to see. The children filled the air with laughter. This brought her lots of hugs. That was thanks enough for Malka.

Leaving now from that little town, Andrew was beginning to understand that Malka's involvement with him was a God-sky. A full God-sky consists of those things that humans can't put their fingers on, but they know that God has heard and is in the mix. They know that sometimes a prayer just prayed, or even previously prayed, always gets answered. Supernatural results in their lives even healings are very strong and Angels unaware are in play.

Andrew loved to start their walks with singing, and sometimes he would dance in the spirit. When Malka tried it, her body just went around and around. She had watched him pray several times—sometimes all night long—and then when he was on her back, he would fall asleep with his head falling forward. During those times, she would just stop for a while. She would gently kneel and let him slide off; then she would watch over him until he awoke. Yes, she dearly loved her master, Andrew.

Sometimes he would look at her as if to say, *Okay, little queen, which way?* That push into the water let him know another side of her. For instance, he began to notice the times when he would hold a child and bless it in the name of the Father, Son, and Holy Ghost that Malka's ears would glow. At other times, while tending to the sick and elderly, when he would gently place someone on Malka's back, he noticed that one ear would twitch. Malka loved doing that for him. God blessed his ministry and multiplied his accomplishments through the Holy Ghost.

Malka would also get a blessing. For you see, she could hear the people thanking God for Andrew. They would be considering that there really was a God. And then they would begin to talk about the new message, the message that the God who created all things loved them.

Several times during the journey to their destination, Malka's passenger would get off her back and walk, sometimes even run. Yes, even a donkey could see the reactions and hear the sounds coming from those whom God blessed. In addition, Malka noticed that at times Andrew would look afar as though he were thinking about something or someone, caring for unknown people: poor, rich, young, old. He looked like he was contemplating all those Gentile countries, all on the outside, but now able to enter in because of the love of God toward all people and the work of His son, Jesus Christ.

Those humans could not hear her inward sensing. They only heard the loud braying and saw her rolling in the grass on her back. If she had been a dog she would have been standing on her hind legs barking for joy and wagging her tail a million wags.

"Thank you, Nicodemus, for sending me to Rome. I have loved every inch of the ground on which we have walked. I have loved every fiber in my tall, caring disciple with a heart of gold." Such a big heart carried well the big vision.

Andrew said to her once, "Queen, if you give up a brother, God will give you a hundred elsewhere." He didn't finish his thought process; he just touched his ear and had a faraway look. When the braying was done, she rolled in the grass as her ears twitched and glowed.

14

The Wedding

T he whole town was buzzing with excitement for the wedding that was to be held Sunday. The bride's parents had already finished the *ohliadyny* (inspection of wealth) and found the bridegroom to be of the highest assessment.

The town now had a reason to celebrate the festivities for at least several days. A wedding meant that some could do the *tsyhanshchyna* (gypsying), the collecting of means for further merrymaking throughout the village. The townspeople knew that weddings meant songs and a magic ritual over all those who chose to join.

Andrew knew some of the wedding traditions of the area from a former visit. The Tkach family had invited him to come back for their daughter's wedding and to help with the marriage ceremony. He wondered if there was going to be a *svashky* (woman's choir) at the ceremony or just silence. He knew that the parents would be giving the *blahoslovlennia* (the pre-wedding blessing) before they departed for the chapel.

"Well, my little queen, the wedding is in this small chapel." Looking at the outside, he was pleased at how nice it looked with the flowers around the outside and neatly manicured shrubbery. "You wait here and don't wander off. I will ask the father to let you carry the bride back to the house for the feast," Andrew conversed to her. So standing like a good donkey, she waited and decided to have a taste of the new flowers, just wanting someone to appreciate them.

Inside the chapel, the scene was lovely, decorated by those who were helping with the greenery and setting up the small tetrapod. It was covered by a *rushnyk* (embroidered cloth) of colorful stitch work by the bride's mother and her friends. The tetrapod was sitting on a lovely rug where the couple would stand in front with the priest behind them. Andrew knew that he did not want to forget to ask them do the *rushnyk* (the dance of Isaiah) three times. Three times also meant the Father, Son, and Holy Spirit, and he knew how Jesus loved and enjoyed himself at the wedding in Cana. He wanted them to know that a circle would not have a break but would be for life.

The bridegroom's relatives arrived at the bride's house to claim her and to take her willingly or unwillingly to the chapel. After the ceremony, Andrew slowly brought Malka alongside the steps of the entrance to the little chapel, and the lovely bride was lifted upon her back along with cheers and flower petals floating on her, as well as on Malka. Andrew and the new husband followed, with the husband walking first alongside his new bride, now his wife. Malka mused, "Weddings, humans surely love those. Everyone laughs and enjoys themselves, but the customs are so different in each place."

Entering the mother's home, they saw the *hiltse viltse*, a ceremonial wreath made up of a green tree with flowers, ribbons, and ears of wheat. The *vinky* (wreath) had periwinkle and birds and yellow flowers. On one table sat the *korovai* (the wedding bread decorated with birds and flowers), waiting for the friend of the couple to cut and divide it for the group. Some of the neighbors donated the flour for its baking.

A table for the placing of the gifts was decorated with a long cross-stitch piece prepared by the bride's great-grandmother. On a long table was a homemade rustic book, which listed the *zaproshuvannia* (all the invited guests). Some just placed the invitation along with a gift whether it was homemade or a special gift or just coins. Outside were tables loaded with food and tables for the guests. All were awaiting the special seating of the couple at the table of order called *posad*. Meanwhile the women were busy placing headbands on their heads to represent decorated wreaths. They wanted to hurry to join in on the fun.

Malka found out that humans can get a little wild, especially when the *kolomeyka* dance started. She had to scurry out of the way in the backyard, for the group had started a strange dance that had the young and old alike weaving crazily, and they were heading right in her direction. A tall, limber gentleman was first, and being a leader, he appeared to be in control of the snakelike line of people. They were trailing behind with hands joined and laughing as they followed him through the open door back into the house; where winding from room to room, laughter of different volumes came forth. Soon the participants encircled the kitchen table, snaked through the living room, and twisted their way around the table and chairs. They danced with laughter, spiraling their way back outside again. Someone had lost a shoe while others dropped their flower-head crowns. Whew, that was a labor of love and fun. *Strange human custom*, thought Malka.

The wedding guests then seated themselves around their own tables. Malka tried to join in the seating celebration and help herself to some food over at the big, loaded feast table, but a little, old maiden shooed her away.

After being seated, the crowd began clapping and singing the *Mnohaya lita* song, which they repeated over and over several times when the best man did the *rozpodil*, the division or cutting and distributing of the wedding bread among the wedding guests. Malka noticed that Andrew had put some of the *korovai* into his pouch after the groom and bride enjoyed the first bite. She wondered if that was for her. Yes, human weddings were certainly nice. Malka remembered Andrew telling her of how he watched Jesus turn water into wine at a wedding in Cana of Galilee.

15

Memories

As one grows older, memories become the sweetness that helps the aging mind. Memories seem never to age though, they just fade with time. Andrew had preached in many cities, such as Byzantium, Thrace, and Patras. Some of finest working memories though were of Neaopolis, where he had erected a cross depicting Jesus's crucifixion, the memory of beautiful people and places that God never forgets. He had also traveled up the Borysthenes River several times, and when he passed by the place where Malka let him have the right nose of fellowship, he would laugh, and then bow his head and thank the God of heaven and earth that He could create such a love and such a bond between man and beast.

Age at last began to affect both Malka and Andrew, each moving more slowly with time. Malka developed a limp; thus was no longer able to keep pace. Andrew remembered the wedding he had performed sometime back, so he took Malka back to the area and asked the young couple if they would be able to take her along with Eleni's colt. They fondly remembered the wedding decorated donkey. Although the couple had no room for two donkeys, they advised Andrew that their Aunt Tkach has a farm with plenty of room. Aunt Tkach was happy to take the pair and promised that both would be treated kindly. She was very glad to be of some kind of service to such a religious, benevolent man like Andrew.

Eleni stayed with Andrew and continued to be a blessing when needed. When leaving the farm, Andrew had an unusual feeling like Lesia knew about this turn of events. He could almost sense her prescience just around the corner. He shrugged off the feeling, however, and went on his way.

Malka enjoyed her early retirement to the lovely ranch-type farm. The grass was green, and her benefactors treated her like the queen she was. Eleni's young colt was blessed as well. Eleni's offspring was notably different from birth. She seemed to be able to open the back door and get out of the barn even though her owners knew they had bolted it tight for the night. Yes, Strange was the given name that Nadia Tkach tagged on that one. Bohdan agreed with his wife that the little one was very different.

16

Rome Revisited

Herodias, getting over a battle with her consumption, was becoming homesick for Jerusalem and feeling better decided she had better move while the weather was good for taking the trip by ship. Herodias, as her usual self, set the whole household in the demand and do mode. Spending the summer eating the delicious fruit and vegetables of Jerusalem was just what would cure anybody of anything were the intelligent remarks made throughout the household.

Lesia could hardly control her hands from shaking, as she packed the trunks, securing each of them by special heavy square locks. Her thoughts were wonderfully mixed, first about going back to Jerusalem and second about not losing one of these trunks or else the wrath of old Hateful would be brought down upon her, whether it was her fault or the ship's. The trip was uneventful except for one small problem the night before docking in Joppa when the crew members' cat crept into the small room and jumped upon old Herodias's small cot during the night. Herodias, thinking that this was an akhbar, screamed and with flaying arms proceeded to knock the startled cat to the floor. The shifting of the ship brought about the rest of the scene to laughable portions. Trying to balance herself with her legs back into the cot while frantically re-straightening her night cap, Herodias fell out of the little cot, landing beside the startled cat with a thud right on her derriere with legs flailing.

"Shoo, you ugly thing. Lesia, where are you? Lesia, get this dreadful, stinky thing out of here."

"Yes, milady." Lesia, stoking the cat's head, noticed it had only one eye. *So sad*, she thought, *but it seemed healthy enough.* "Go, little one. Get… shoo, shoo."

Lesia adjusted the covers back over Herodias, who was soon fast asleep and snoring, dreaming dreams of ruling the world. Lesia spent her dreams, dreaming of being with Andrew. The summer cottage was a delightful change from the Roman openness.Thecourtyards with their marble inlaid were spectacular but nothing compared to the open markets of Jerusalem. The smell and sounds of the marketplace pounded in her bloodstream, as years drifted away and memories swept over her, churning her inner being, stealing her away to the fish peddler and his love. A sigh brought her back to reality—no, things had changed, and so had Jerusalem.

Unexpectedly, Herodias had another scare, her coughing this time sounding more serious. Three months of this coughing caused Lesia to start feeling a change of heart toward old Hateful.

One morning after bath time, Herodias asked Lesia to bring her a special red box from her personal belongings. Herodias fingered the box greedily then opened it. She pulled out some papers and one folded envelope, telling Lesia that when the time came, this whole box was to be hers. Speaking in a weak moment, Herodias revealed that Mara Chin had sent a special envelope to Rome, instructing that it was to be given to Lesia upon his death. This event had totally slipped Herodias's mind until just now when she opened the box and spied the envelope.

Still musing in this weakened condition, Herodias proceeded to also state, "The coins and jewelry will help you when you are a free woman." Coughing again, she expressed with her hand Lesia's dismissal from the room, while keeping the box and the letter with her. Old Hateful in control again. Lesia shook off her desire to have the envelope now. *Where is Mara Chin?* she wondered. *Didn't Herodias not mention that I was to get the letter upon Mara Chin's death? Is he dead or alive? I haven't been able to find him or any news of him.*

Like so many other times when Lesia wanted something so badly, she would be denied, Herodias always reminding her of her enslavedness, her freedom an ever-dangling carrot before her. Old Hateful used freedom as a ploy, cruel to the core, "Yes, maybe today I will free you, but then, on the other hand, maybe we should wait until tomorrow, shouldn't we, dear?" Then some meaningless task, like sitting and fanning her for an hour, would be assigned to Lesia. Hateful was true to her colors.

Someday, Lesia thought, she would be free, but for now she was back in Jerusalem, the lovely city of her childhood with fond memories of Mara Chin and his kindness as a loving parent. Little did she know that Mara Chin was now visiting in Athens, Greece.

The next few days were wonderful in the city. The fruit and the vegetables were the best this year. Herodias, to Lesia's surprise, also began to respond to the warmer climate. Lesia went several places to find out if Andrew had returned or if anyone knew anything about him. As luck would have it, she ran into John Mark and his mother Mary. Andrew had mentioned them many times. She and the household of Herodias also knew about Mary since she was a well-known lady of means in the business arena and was well thought of by the townspeople. Several times Lesia returned to the house of Mary and John Mark when other Christians were there. The discussions about the Gospel of Christ that incurred were dynamic and genuine, moving Lesia more and more into understanding why Andrew gave up his worldly desires and accepted the commission to preach. When around these Christians, it seemed easier for Lesia to believe, and she would leave the meeting with a greater head knowledge of the Gospel message, little knowing that a closer encounter was around the corner for her.

John Mark was so grown up, and his devotion to his mother portrayed a tender scene. John Mark mentioned that from what they had heard, Andrew had gone to Rome and was able see Peter. He then went north, and it was thought that he traveled through Greece and the area of the Black Sea as well. It was also told that he had a side kick with him, a small donkey, which had some questionable behavior.

Inside her heart beat this message, "Oh, my beloved. Will life give me another chance to behold your wonderful face and strong smile before I die? When my chance comes, I will search for you until I take my last breath. I feel that chance is as close now as ever!"

The whole household was again set in motion, for Nero was hosting another one of his parties, and this time Herodias herself was invited. "Herodias, you can't be for real that you want to attend this gala that Nero is throwing for everyone that is anyone back in Rome. You may not be strong enough yet for the crossing," Lesia told her. This advice, however, fell on deaf ears. Nero was Herodias' god. Strong, old Hateful was herself again, so once more clothes were washed and repacked. Personal belongings, including the red box, were returned to the trunks. Lesia was still unaware of what was in the letter that was in the possession of old Hateful as it remained locked away.

The skyline of Rome was a gala for sure, but this time Rome was burning and not the dear Christians or the animals Nero would choose for his games. Chaos reigned as panicked people were unsure where to go. Lesia quickly grabbed an empty bag then ran to search for the key to unlock the red box that was so important—important enough to be taken and taken now. Freedom also, why not—it's now or never. With heart pounding and nerves on edge, the search proved to be futile; the key could not be found. So the whole red box was placed into the bag. She hoped that the fire would burn the whole little palace down around old Hateful's things, things that she worships. Hardly expressing that feeling deep inside her, she began to now hear the people's screams, "Look, the fire is growing and our chance for safety is to go toward the sea. Get out of the city." As she hurried, she found herself mingled in a sea all right, but not a sea of water, rather a sea of people, panicked and fearful. She must not fall lest she would get another kind of freedom. To survive the turmoil, instinct took over and was on everyone's agenda, each pushing the person in front and in back so that distance was put between each one and the fire.

Smoke and cinders now filled the air, distributing over the city by a rapid wind that flowed during the evening hours. The hot cinders knew well what to do when they fell upon rooftops or dry grass. A heavy blanket of death was at each ones' heels, everyone running, not walking.

As morning came, and the day grew on so was the reality of what had happened. Lesia saw that a ship was near, and without any thought, she ran up the gangplank along with many others that had the same thing in mind, getting away from here, away from a destroyed city. She wiped back her tears and shoved along with the others so that the captain finally pulled up the gangplank and ordered that one sail be hoisted in order for the ship to drift away from the dock. Finding a secluded spot where she felt that she could bang the red box down sideways against the lock hinge, she hoped to open it. Yes, it fell sideways and opened.

Lesia slipped out a red ruby brooch. Ah, what a good bird in the hand this proved to be, and it got her a small separate nook near the captain's cabin in the lower deck. She was surprised but thought that it was all right that this ship was going to Greece. She felt that destiny was handing her the map to start her search for Andrew. Little did she know that it would also restart her life.

17

Greece

In Athens, Greece, Lesia had been working for a few months cooking, child sitting, and laundering, giving her only a few precious moments at a time to inquire about Andrew. Searching for Andrew had always been the driving force of her life, the primary goal above all other wants and desires, since that day when she was forced travel to Rome. After reading the letter from the red box, she had pledged to herself that if Andrew was found her next goal would be to find out about her people. For now though, she only would take short-term employments so that she could keep searching for Andrew before facing what she had to do about the news of her childhood. Sometimes, she would find a connection. Yes, villagers would tell her, a tall preacher man was here. He helped many people and miracles were manifested among the village, but he left saying he was following his music and could not stay any longer. Some even talked about the strange donkey that was with him. They mentioned that he was like a phantom, always on the move.

Finally, the break Lesia was looking for came her way. Her latest employer, Kara DeStefano, the mother of three children, mentioned that a Christian movement was happening in the little town bar down by the dock. A sailor told a story about a new teaching that was connected with the Jews. An ill person was healed and began witnessing to anyone who would listen, telling everyone about salvation through Jesus. Bishop Ben had arrived with news of the events occurring up north.

Lesia later found herself down at the wharf looking for Bishop Ben. She found him, and he told her about the tall preacher man that had been in a village up north in Berea. He did miracles among the villagers but soon left saying he was following his music and could not stay any longer. Some even talked about the strange donkey that was with him. They mentioned that he was like a phantom, always on the move. Hearing again the same story about the donkey and he was like a phantom- meant to her heart and mind- a sense- he is lonesome- lack of companion- he is still unmarried.

159

This mind sense secret shared within her heart- he still was her soul mate. Yes, Andrew you know I know. Bishop Ben had heard that more believers were in Patras, so he is getting ready to go there to see if he could join them and learn more about this new movement. He would be heading for the west side of Greece in a few days after he connected with an old sea dog, who would usually get drunk and miss his ship.

Early on the third day, Leisa was all excited. She wondered why she hadn't thought of looking for them—Christians that was their new name. Bishop Ben met her at the end of garden gate early that morning to begin their journey to Patras, thirty-four miles all by foot. Bishop Ben had water with him but knew that Athens was growing by leaps and bounds and was confident they would find a place to stop if need be. He was quiet, however, disappointed that he had not connected with his old drinking partner Mugface from shipping days. He had such a Good News message for him.

Lesia had said her good-byes to the family the previous evening, especially to the child that had a speech problem. He was a very sweet boy and even when he tried hard to speak, he still could not form his words like his siblings could. She held him for a while longer as she could see that his eyes were now full of tears another reason to leave very early before the whole family awoke and she had to go through her good-byes again. She rechecked to make sure she had all her belongings. Inside herself was a nervousness and yet an excitement as well since she would be searching for her soul mate.

Leisa let Bishop Ben take the lead on the way, and with his long strides she found herself a little behind him. Finally, the silence became too much for her, and she began talking about Andrew and her love for him. Before long, several miles and several hours had gone by. They finally stopped by a little old stone hut to rest. The occupant had settled with her ailing sea captain years ago. "Good day to yar," the old woman said as she welcomed them with a hand gesture toward the water bucket. The old lady's thoughts were, yippee, rubbing her hands together. She was glad that many travelers used this path, which went right past her little cottage. It was good for pickings. "Leave a little something for the water bucket." Conveying a hint, she shook the little box and placed it nearby.

Bishop Ben and Leisa did not mind and tossed a coin into the small box beside the water bucket. Then they found out the water was wine. By morning the old lady had heard about the wine that Jesus used as He offered a new covenant to twelve Jewish men in an upper room in Jerusalem.

Bishop Ben was no worse for the wear without sleep and again his long strides kept up a good pace for hours. By mid-afternoon on a bright warm day, they arrived in a small lower section of Patras where they found another quaint inn, with the possibility of a job for Leisa. Bishop Ben had friends in the upper part of north Patras, so he hugged Leisa good-bye, promising that if he heard anything about Andrew, he would return with the news for her.

18

Slave for Life

Andrew continued to see the workings of the Lord. Many came to believe, and many were healed. Yes, he was called in that vision, the vision filled with music, so long ago to places that were like him (fourth man out without direction). He was not backward in preaching about sin, having the mannerism of John the Baptist who verbally spewed forth like the fire from a dragon.

Yes, he may have been quiet in his youth, but now as he was faced with death on a cross of his own, he was strong in Spirit. He remained very vocal for two days while dying. Yes, he was very, very vocal for the Good News. His love came forth for the Messiah, and it thundered without raining.

Some covered their ears; others found their Messiah in those two days. Over at a small farm in the back in a small field, the donkeys, along with the other farm animals, became quiet.

Lesia stood a distance away and watched the crowd. The crowd was watching "the fourth man out" dying. For two days, Andrew had kept on preaching the Good News. "Repent," he preached from the cross; the cross made like an *X*.

The town people kept begging for Andrew's release, calling for the authorities to untie him and get him down. "No," cried Andrew. "Should I not drink the cup that is mine?" Lesia moved closer to observe what was happening and was on the outskirts of the crowd. It was then she overheard people saying, "He has no whelps. Who will get his belongings?"

She pressed in more quickly and began asking, "Who is he? Who is it that is on the cross?"

"My fair lady," sobbed an elderly man, "it is our beloved apostle, Andrew."

Then someone else, crying and holding her face, was sobbing, "Our sweet Andrew, our precious disciple."

There were no words to tell how her insides groaned as she bit her lip. "My life was never to marry, always to be a slave. This cross, Andrew, was so very heavy. Daily I had to face the burden of never being able to marry or bear children unless Hateful would decide to sell me." Adjusting her feelings and her thoughts while wiping away her tears, she continued her lament. "But why should I be crying about my life. I traveled. I had nice things. And, Andrew, look at what you, my beloved, just went through—a cross of death, a cross meant to shame you. Andrew, I should not be complaining about myself today. I hang on no cross except the cross in my heart. Your death showed that you loved to the end for the sake of the kingdom. King Jesus was your friend as well as your Master. You just suffered for the kingdom."

"I am so proud of you. I now realize that the things I heard about a caring, compassionate preacher, the stories of healing, of miracles, and of love for children, was you. I have also heard about the legend that has arisen about you. The saying states that if a person would let the priest eat and stay at his house, his daughters and sons will all marry. Andrew, God is so very proud of you. I know where you are, so rest my beloved. Your work is done."

The crowd began to disperse; the sadness was beyond belief as each one headed toward his or her own hut and some down to the village pub. She then noticed an elderly couple*** standing at the foot of the cross. That aging couple was weeping at the demoralizing cross****. She followed them as they tenderly carried Andrew's body away toward their home. She approached the couple and explained that she knew Andrew a long time ago. Weeping, they told her why he died. They said that Andrew wanted to put up a cross to honor the Lord. Aegeates***** was so infuriated that he had their beloved Andrew tortured and killed.

Lesia asked to see him. As she stepped closer, she stopped. What was causing the glow? She tenderly lifted the burial cloth to say a good-bye. She wept. Andrew's ear was glowing. She touched her ear. Her slave for life earring was gone now. Free. Yes, and so was her beloved. Little did she know that her ear glowed with the enduring light of, like Andrew, a slave for life to the Gospel of Jesus Christ.

Andrew was now free to hear, "Welcome home, my good and faithful servant. He that endures to the end will be saved."

"Enduring, Andrew, I am." She turned and left with un-described sadness within her, but still whispered as she touched her ear, "I am enduring, Andrew, my soul mate forever. I will endure to the end. Her spiritual earring glowed, unseen by her or the world. The seeds of faith planted by Andrew, Mary, and John Mark were now planted in her soul. Would they take root and grow deeper, maturing her to the see more of this picture of Jesus and His kingdom. So far having the dream of reuniting with Andrew was the force of her enduring, but would she remain strong? Without the physical force of her love for Andrew, would she have enough strength to continue believing if she should face a life or death situation? It was the unseen force, his love for Jesus that kept him enduring. Lesia felt that she lacked maturity and an unexplainable confidence.

The weeping elderly couple both in unison said, "We want you to have his sandals to give to a deserving person, if you can." Hmm, looking at them, she said almost as a whisper, "They look like he must have just bought them, but they seem to be more Roman than Scythian. Yes, I will give them to someone, I promise," and gave them both a hug.

She looked back once more at that ugly cross, really alone this time with lonely thoughts within her head and heart. She could no longer talk to Andrew face-to-face, the dream that kept giving her inner strength ended here today. She couldn't tell him anything verbally anymore: the burning of Rome, the horror, her lonely nights in a small, overcrowded ship. He would never know of the Mara Chin letter with the locket, how excited she was to be out of Herodias's sight and even the sound of her voice. Lesia's excitement concerning that day played over and over in her head and helped drive her on. Yes, but most of all she wanted to tell him again about her love, her crazy crush of love, which happened the first time she saw him that day he spilled the fish.

She wondered what he would have told her about the adventures he had gone through and the experiences he had had with different people and different cultures. However, she knew that his love for her still continued even though it was in second place.

Her steps were slow ones now as she talked to herself while going down the path to head south to the harbor. Sighing and sniffing, she wiped her eyes again; then one strong thought came to her, "Yes, I didn't get to share all my thoughts with him, but I am so glad that life gave me the opportunity to place a kiss on his cheek in a final good-bye. Yes, in my heart of hearts, I know that he knew." Inside her being was a sure confident feeling that when it came to Andrew, he knew.

"Enduring, Andrew, I am." She turned to leave and whispered as she touched her ear. "I am enduring, Andrew, my soul mate forever. I will endure to the end. Her spiritual earring glowed, unseen by the world.

Just then a very strong breeze caught her hair and brushed it briskly around her face and ears, twirling vigorously around her dress, energetically around her body and legs, her shawl blowing straight off her shoulders. Then, quietness. It was a brief moment of a hug from God's creation, the wind. Smiling, she thanked the God of Andrew because way back in Jerusalem she began believing in her head when Andrew talked and talked about Jesus. Now she believed in her heart.

"I guess I should be like Bishop Ben, who came with me from Athens, wanting more truth." She decided to say this prayer, "Thank you, God. You hear the faintest prayer and see the faintest heartache. Yes, you are aware of all our fears and short comings. Thank you for the wind hug. It made me remember what Andrew once told me about the time of the great wind on the stormy Sea of Galilee. He said they all cried out thinking they had seen a ghost coming through the troubled sea, but it was Jesus, Jesus whom the wind and the sea obeyed. Jesus who saved them from the storm now will help me in these trying days ahead. Andrew talked about keeping the Faith. I must trust God."

A little donkey with one ear that at times twitched and glowed began to follow Lesia, and she turned several times to shoo it away. "Go back to your owner, little one," she said. But it wouldn't leave her side and just kept walking as close as it could. "You win, little one, and this bundle is very heavy, so I will let you help." The right ear of the donkey began to glow.

The donkey stopped and received the bundle. Lesia let the animal continue walking with her and for some odd reason began to pour out her feelings to it. "I need to find my family, little one. I didn't think I would stumble upon Andrew like it happened, but for some reason when Andrew needed to hear from me or I needed to hear from him, it was as if we had a messenger angel between us. You can't imagine, little donkey, in this human heart and body that the inner part can love and love even when two people are so far apart. It would be like we'd know something but didn't have the evidence in our sight. I guess it was intuition, having inner thoughts about each other.

Turning to the donkey, she said, "My sweet one, I think I will call you— let me see— Ahava. I am sad, but inside I am full of faith and love. So I will call you Ahava (love)."

Yes, thought Ahava, *my lineage will now continue. I will help her, for you see, love will see her home.*

Inside Lesia's bundle were her mother's locket and a small note. She was returning to the place where she as a baby had been given to a traveling couple that was fleeing the vicinity because of the plague. Lesia's mother had handed her small baby over to them, hoping to spare her child from the dreaded disease. The note and locket had come to Rome addressed from the family of Mara Chin. The note began: Precious child. It told her who she was.

Lesia readjusted her shawl and placed Andrew's sandals into the saddle bag. She noticed this time a sweet fragrance that seemed to be on them; maybe they had been anointed with oil. She patted Ahava's nose and placed her arms around her neck to readjust the rope. "Little one, Ahava," softly speaking, "guess we had better get started. We will need to find a place to sleep before dark."

Ahava expressed the ending the best way she could. Or perhaps it was the beginning.

Andrews's sandals were singing. Lesia couldn't hear, but Ahava could.

"Silly donkey, why are you braying? And why all this turning and turning around?"

*   same meaning/temple/synagogue

**   note to teachers, readers, students Christian Computer Art www.cc-Art.com

Pictures speak a thousand words
Bible Picture Gallery
They have over 6,000+Images
Check the ancient windows
Please visit and enjoy.
Pattern for kids to do a hut.

***   Research:

- Order of St. Andrew the Apostle ARCHONS OF THE ECUMENICAL PATRIARCHATE
- Bishop Stratoklis and Maximilla.
- Bishop Stratoklis was high intellectual brother of the Proconsul, he also became a Christian and before Andrew's death he was made first Bishop of Patras.
- Aegeates' wife is: Maximilla who was healed and converted. Andrew was buried in her tomb.

****   CROSS WAS CALLED DECUSSATE

*****   Aegeates realized that the man he had put to death was truly a holy man of God his conscience became so tormented that he committed suicide.

Addendum

Go Ye Therefore

Mary Stanton is a retired Algebra instructor and Bible teacher. Now she enjoys reading and tending to her multiple flower beds.

As the disciples heeded Jesus' command given in Matthew 28:19, "Go ye therefore, and teach all nations…," the Gospel message began to spread into all the world. It was said of Paul and Silas, "These that have turned the world upside down are come hither also" (Acts 17:6). One might ask, "Where did the disciples go? What were these lands like in the first century? What would we see today?"

It is believed that Andrew preached primarily in areas around the Black Sea and up the Dnieper River. He may have traveled as far as Spain and Scotland as well. Most authorities accept that he was martyred in Patras, Greece. In our story, Andrew travels to the territories of Kiev, Donetsk, and Odessa in modern day Ukraine; Thrace on the western shore of the Black Sea, now Bulgaria; Byzantium, southwest of the Black Sea, currently Istanbul, Turkey; and Patras, located in Greece. He didn't have modern transportation that would convey him to these places in a matter of hours over the one-thousand-mile- plus journey. No, he traveled by foot, lovingly and without complaint, to carry the Good News of the Gospel message to a lost and dying world.

In the time of Andrew's travels, there were no large cities. The region of his travels was dotted with colonies from several people groups. Prior to Jesus time, the Scythians populated northern areas of modern Ukraine, while Greek colonists had ventured out into areas surrounding the Black Sea. By the time Jesus traveled the area of Israel, the Roman Empire ruled the region. During Roman rule, many roads were established, travel had become safer, and urban areas began to be expanded. Compared to the more advanced, wealthy, and urban eastern part of the empire, the western section was little more than backward, tribal groupings. The Romans were instrumental in advancing the European continent into becoming the modern western culture it is today.

Geographically, Southern Ukraine toward the Black Sea is a flat, treeless plain called a steppe region, while Central Ukraine is forest covered with the Carpatean Mountains located to the west. The area is inundated with water, bearing seventy-three thousand streams and rivers, and twenty thousand lakes. Many of these waters are mineral springs; thus the Ukraine is noted for its medical and therapeutic treatments.

The region's climate is moderate with mild winters not producing any severe frosts; however, regular snowfall occurs and rivers and lakes freeze, except in the southern region. Because of the favorable climatic conditions and fertile, black soil, the Ukraine is a traditional agricultural area, producing barley, maize, potatoes, rice, soybeans, sugar beets, and wheat.

Kiev, the capital, a center of business and commerce, is the largest city in Ukraine, with a mixed population of over two and a half million people. There is an estimated 130 nationalities living within the urban area.

The city spans both eastern and western sides of the Dnieper River. Historians believe that the region was inhabited as early as the second century and certainly by the sixth century. The older western side of the city is inundated with woody hills and many ravines, small rivers, and lakes. A total of 448 bodies of water, both natural and manmade, lie within its borders.

Further east of Kiev, Donetsk is Ukraine's fifth largest city, located on the Kalmius River. The city was founded in 1869 by John Hughes, a Welsh business man, who opened coal mines in the area and built a steel mill. It was named Yuzoyka for Hughes, whose name in Russian is Yuz. During the reign of Stalin the name was changed to Stalin and later to Stalino. In 1961, during the anti-Stalin era, the city name became Donetsk, named after the Seversky Donets River. Today, Donetsk is a leading industrial city with many ironworks, rails, coal mines, coking plants, machinery works, and chemical plants. Because of the favorable river conditions, annual sailboat championships are held here, as well.

Two hundred seventy-five miles south of Kiev, located on the northwest shore of the Black Sea, is the city of Odessa, the fourth largest of Ukraine. Greeks were the earliest colonists of the region. Later, it became a Tatar settlement founded by Haci I Siray in 1270. The city was originally named

Hacibey for Haci. The modern city was established by order of Catherine the Great in 1794. By the 1800s many diverse people lived in the region. It is situated on terraced hills overlooking the Black Sea, nineteen miles north of an estuary of the Dniester River.

Odessa is a major port city, exporting oil and chemicals. These facilities are connected to Russia and Europe by a series of pipelines and rails.

The area known in Bible times as Thrace had no definite boundaries. The Balkan Mountains were located to the north with the Black Sea to the east and Macedonia to the southwest. The majority of the region today lies within the borders of Bulgaria with Greece claiming the western portion and Turkey some of the eastern section. Climatically, the area is hot and humid in the summer and cold, wet, and often snowy in the winter. The region also tends to be windy. Crops produced on its rich, black soil include corn, sunflower seeds, winter wheat, and winter barley.

An important modern day city, Istanbul, was settled by Greek colonists in 667 BC. An early name was Byzantium, later changed to Constantinople in honor of its famous ruler Constantine. In 1930, the name changed once again, becoming Istanbul, which is now the capital of Turkey.

Istanbul is located on a peninsula on the Bosporus Straight, the entrance from the Black Sea to the Sea of Marmara. This region forms a natural protection from invading enemies. Today, Istanbul is the largest city in Turkey and the third largest city in Europe with a population of over thirteen million people. The city spans both sides of the Bosporus, causing it to be located on two continents, both Europe and Asia. Istanbul is built on seven hills; however, it lies upon a fault line and has experienced numerous earthquakes, some with devastating consequences.

Greece is a peninsula extending from the Balkans, formerly known as Macedonia, to the Mediterranean Sea. The area is mountainous with many gulfs and bays. Much of the land is stony; however, some is suitable for growing and produces wheat, barley, citrus, dates, and olives. The climate is predominately Mediterranean with hot, dry summers and mild, wet winters. The rainy season lasts from October to March.

Geographically, Greece is divided into three regions: northern Greece, central Greece, and the Peloponnese. The Peloponnese is almost entirely surrounded by water, connected to central Greece by a natural land bridge, the Isthmus of Corinth.

Patras, a thriving port city, and the main source of export for Peloponnese agriculture is believed to be the site of Andrew's martyrdom. It is located in the foothills of Mount Panachaikon on the northern coast overlooking the Gulf of Patras.

Patras is an ancient city, dating back four thousand years. The area is noted for its frequent, almost daily seismic activity with more destructive earthquakes occurring every few years. Over the centuries, Patras has grown into the third largest urban area in Greece, supporting a population of close to half a million residents in its combined urban and metropolitan areas. It is built on two levels due to its natural geography and the architectural plans for its immense population and is connected by a series of stairs. The lower section on the coast was built on a bed of river soils and dried-up swamps. The upper, older area is an elevated section built around the base of the Fortress on Mount Panachaikon.

As Andrew traversed the area, he navigated waterways, climbed mountains, and journeyed through valleys and ravines, encountering many people and spreading the Gospel message on his way. In modern times the area has greatly changed, expanding in both development of the land and population growth. With all its modernity, however, it is as much in need of the Gospel message today as it was in Andrew's time.

GOD SKY II

Available soon!!!

About the Author

Pearl M. Smithern born the fifth child (August 18th, 1936) to Charles Allen Smithern and Sarah Ann Correll. Times were depression with food stamps and war.

She remembers her mother having her be quiet while listening to the President on a small old brown radio and then praying for her brother Clyde in the Navy. (Feb. 1943 enlisted in Cleveland, Ohio)

August 18, 1936 Pearl was named after her father's sister. Pearl started school at 6 years of age at Suffield Grade School- half of her third year started at Roosevelt Grade School, Akron-twelfth grade graduated 16th in her class at Springfield high- 1954. Summer was earning credits from Hammel Business School downtown Akron, and working for Superior Staffing on clerical jobs. Married on December 14th, 1954. Later a data entry degree in Greensboro, NC- Rutledge College.

Pearl has been in children's ministries since the age of fifteen, where she helped her mother clean a little church and began a love for God.

Both parents are from Kentucky, Kidder, Wayne county and Woodstock, Pulaski county. Her father was born in 1900 and at the age of twenty came to Akron, Ohio to work at a new rubber plant called Goodyear. Her father went back for Sarah- born 1903- and moved to a farm 1926 located in Portage County, Suffield Ohio.

Picture in front of school, Suffield, Ohio

www.ingramcontent.com/pod-product-compliance
Lightning Source LLC
Chambersburg PA
CBHW040844120626
46547CB00001B/22